Erwin Dee Kord (Ed.)

Web Inquiry Projects

Erwin Dee Kord (Ed.)

Web Inquiry Projects

San Diego State University, University of Illinois at Urbana–Champaign, Information

Solv

Imprint

Permission is granted to copy, distribute and/or modify this document under the terms of the GNU Free Documentation License, Version 1.2 or any later version published by the Free Software Foundation; with no Invariant Sections, with the Front-Cover Texts, and with the Back- Cover Texts. A copy of the license is included in the section entitled "GNU Free Documentation License".

All parts of this book are extracted from Wikipedia, the free encyclopedia (www.wikipedia.org).

You can get detailed informations about the authors of this collection of articles at the end of this book. The editors (Ed.) of this book are no authors. They have not modified or extended the original texts.

Pictures published in this book can be under different licences than the GNU Free Documentation License. You can get detailed informations about the authors and licences of pictures at the end of this book.

The content of this book was generated collaboratively by volunteers. Please be advised that nothing found here has necessarily been reviewed by people with the expertise required to provide you with complete, accurate or reliable information. Some information in this book maybe misleading or wrong. The Publisher does not guarantee the validity of the information found here. If you need specific advice (f.e. in fields of medical, legal, financial, or risk management questions) please contact a professional who is licensed or knowledgeable in that area.

Any brand names and product names mentioned in this book are subject to trademark, brand or patent protection and are trademarks or registered trademarks of their respective holders. The use of brand names, product names, common names, trade names, product descriptions etc. even without a particular marking in this works is in no way to be construed to mean that such names may be regarded as unrestricted in respect of trademark and brand protection legislation and could thus be used by anyone.

Cover image: www.ingimage.com
Concerning the licence of the cover image please contact ingimage.

Publisher:
Solv is a trademark of
International Book Market Service Ltd., 17 Rue Meldrum, Beau Bassin, 1713-01 Mauritius
Email: info@bookmarketservice.com
Website: www.bookmarketservice.com

Published in 2012

Printed in: U.S.A., U.K., Germany. This book was not produced in Mauritius.

ISBN: 978-613-9-00010-4

Contents

Web_Inquiry_Projects

Web Inquiry Projects (WIPs) are "open inquiry learning activities that leverage the use of uninterpreted online data and information." They were invented at San Diego State University in 2001.

One example is the University of Illinois at Urbana-Champaign's Ethnography of the University [1] (EOTU) program, which sponsors undergraduate research on the university and archives it in web-accessible form for the UIUC community. EOTU also functions as a learning group for students, staff, and faculty interested in what it means to conduct research on universities as institutions. EOTU understands that universities and colleges—their institutions, organizations, maps, and histories—are composites of diverse prose, visual, network, and statistical narratives.

External links

- The main WIP web site [2] - At this site are examples of teacher-created WIPs, templates for those wishing to create their own WIPs, and a broader discussion of web-based inquiry learning.

References

[1] http://www.eotu.uiuc.edu/
[2] http://edweb.sdsu.edu/wip

San_Diego_State_University

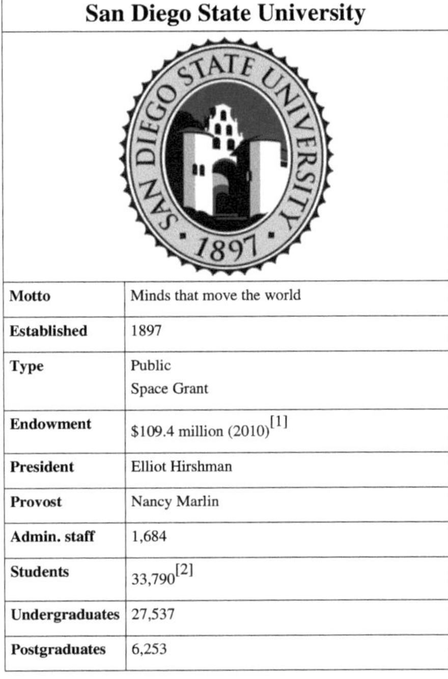

San Diego State University	
Motto	Minds that move the world
Established	1897
Type	Public Space Grant
Endowment	$109.4 million (2010)[1]
President	Elliot Hirshman
Provost	Nancy Marlin
Admin. staff	1,684
Students	33,790[2]
Undergraduates	27,537
Postgraduates	6,253

Location	San Diego, California
Campus	Urban
Former names	San Diego Normal School (1897–1923) San Diego Teachers College (1923–35) San Diego State College (1935–72) California State University, San Diego (1972–74)
Colors	black, scarlet (red), and gold
Athletics	17 varsity teams
Nickname	Aztecs
Mascot	Aztec warrior
Affiliations	California State University system Mountain West Conference (NCAA Division 1)
Website	www.sdsu.edu [3]

San Diego State University (SDSU), founded in 1897 as San Diego Normal School, is the largest and oldest higher education facility in the greater San Diego area (generally the City and County of San Diego), and is part of the California State University system. It is the third-oldest university in the California State University system, and one of the oldest universities in California. SDSU has a student body of approximately 29,256 (as of the beginning of the Fall 2009 academic year) and an alumni base of more than 200,000. San Diego State University received nearly 60,000 undergraduate applications for the 2011 Fall semester.[4] The school accepted 14,480 high school seniors and 2,748 transfers with an acceptance rate of 28.7% for the 2011 academic year.[5]

The Carnegie Foundation has designated San Diego State University a "Research University with high research activity." SDSU is the only California State University campus with this classification, which places it among the top 200 higher education institutions in the country conducting research.[6] Notably, pursuant to the *Faculty Scholarly Productivity Index* (FSP Index) released by the Academic Analytics organization of Stony Brook, NY, SDSU is the number one small research university in the United States as of the last four (4) academic years, from 2005-2006 through the 2009-2010 academic years.[7] [8] [9] [10] In 2010, *The Daily Beast* ranked SDSU No.21 in its list of "Tech's 29 Most Powerful Colleges."[11]

San Diego State University awards bachelor's, master's, and doctoral degrees Ph.D. (jointly with UCSD), Ed.D, and Au.D, in a total of 151 fields. SDSU offers the most doctoral degrees of any campus of the California State University system, currently in sixteen academic and research disciplines.

San Diego State University is a member of the American Association of State Colleges and Universities (AASCU), the National Association of State Universities and Land-Grant Colleges, the Southwest Border Security Consortium, and the Oak Ridge Associated Universities, a national organization of universities that promotes science and technology education and research.

History

Established on March 13, 1897, San Diego State University first began as the **San Diego Normal School**, meant to educate local future female elementary school teachers. In 1923, the San Diego Normal School became **San Diego State Teachers College**, "a four-year public institution controlled by the state Board of Education." In 1935, the school became **San Diego State College.** In 1960, San Diego State College became a part of the California College System, now known as the California State University system. Finally in 1970 San Diego State College became San Diego State University (SDSU).

One in seven San Diegans with a college degree attended SDSU,[12] making SDSU a primary educator of the region's work force. Committed to serving the diverse San Diego region, SDSU ranks among the top ten universities nationwide in terms of ethnic and racial diversity among its student body, as well as the number of bachelor's degrees conferred upon minority students.[12]

San Diego State University has been designated a "Research University" by the Carnegie Foundation.[13] University faculty consistently attract hundreds of millions of U.S. dollars annually in grants and contracts for research and program administration, and SDSU's research and graduate degree programs lead all other campuses of the California State University system.[12] In the 2009-10 academic year, the university obtained $150 million for research, including $26 million from the National Institutes of Health.[14]

For the beginning of the 2006-2007 academic year, SDSU expanded its classrooms and support space by more than 200000 square feet (19000 m^2) with the opening of three new buildings, the College of Arts and Letters, the Calpulli Center and BioScience Center. The buildings, respectively, feature high-technology classrooms, upgraded health and wellness facilities, and scientific research laboratories.

SDSU's Astronomy Department owns the Mount Laguna Observatory located in the Cleveland National Forest. It operates the observatory concurrently with the University of Illinois at Urbana-Champaign.[15]

John F. Kennedy, then the President of the United States of America, gave the graduation commencement address at San Diego State University on June 6, 1963.[16] [17] [18] [19]

> ❝As a nation, we have no deeper concern, no older commitment and no higher interest than a strong, sound and free system of education for all. In fulfilling this obligation to ourselves and our children, we provide for the future of our nation-and for the future of freedom. ❞
> (Historical Video) [20]
>
> —John F. Kennedy, President of the United States of America, Graduation commencement address to San Diego State College (San Diego, California), June 6, 1963

Campus

Several buildings are listed on the National Register of Historic Places:[21]

- Scripps Cottage was finished in September 1931, funded with a donation of $6,000 from Ellen Browning Scripps matched with $5,000 from the state. It was the headquarters for the Associated Women Students and was used for meetings, women's activities, and served as a lounge.[22] On September 3, 1968 the building was moved to make room for the new library. It was used mainly as a conference and meeting building, and in 1993, began serving as a center for international students.[23]

- Aztec Bowl, costing $500,000, the stadium was dedicated on October 3, 1936 before 7,500 people, after being completed earlier that year. The stadium was initially supposed to be expanded to 45,000 seats, but instead was only expanded once with 5,000 seats in 1948. Aztec Bowl was the only state college stadium in California at the time of its construction.[24]

- Open Air Theatre contained 4,280 seats and was financed by the Works Progress Administration and the state for $200,000. It was dedicated in 1941.[25]

- On January 19, 1976, the Montezuma Mesa building was renamed to Walter R. Hepner Hall, and on May 1, 1977 the humanities building was named after John Adams, a teacher, administrator, and archivist. The Humanities-Social Sciences building was renamed in 1986 after geographer Alvena Storm and historian Abraham P. Nasatir.[26]

- In the 1980s the Open Air Theatre added new support facilities and fencing. Peterson Gym was finished in 1961, making the original gym the Women's Gym until it was remodeled and reopened in 1990 as the Physical Education building. In 1990, 14000 sq ft (1300 m^2) were added to Storm and Nasatir Halls. In 1986, a large student apartment complex was added along with a 11-story $13,000,000 residence hall (west side of campus).[27]

- Hardy Memorial Tower, in the Mission Revival style, resembles a Mediterranean church tower and is one of the most recognizable buildings on campus. It also performed a utilitarian function: The tower concealed a 5000 gallon water tank that provided pressure for the campus plumbing system. The building housed the university's first library, which featured murals painted by the Works Progress Administration.[28]

- The Communications Building, Exercise & Nutritional Sciences, Faculty Staff Club, Life Science Building and Annex, Little Theatre, Physical Plant Boiler Shop, and the Physical Science Building are also listed on the National Register.[21]

Other buildings on campus include:

- The campus library, now known as the Malcolm A. Love Library, acquired its 100,000th book on May 21, 1944. By the end of World War II it was adding about 8,000 books a year.[29] In 1959, a 40000 sq ft (3700 m^2). addition to the library was finished, but it was already deemed too small.[30] In 1952, the library had 125,000 books, and state regulations required that old books be eliminated before new ones could be added. By 1965, there were more than 300,000 books housed in a library that could hold 230,000. This was ranked highest in state colleges in terms of library size. In the 1960s, construction of a new library

The front entrance to Love Library

began, which required the relocation of Scripps Cottage. The $8,000,000 building was designed with 300000 sq ft (28000 m^2). of space to accommodate one million books.[31] In February 1971, the library opened, housing 700,000 books, and was named after President Malcolm A. Love for his popularity on campus and his role in bringing State to university status.[32] Governor Ronald Reagan said the library would "...serve as a lasting memorial to the man who led the college through its growing pains...to one of the finest state colleges in California."[33] The building was five stories high and was the largest building on campus. A four-story sculpture entitled "Hanging Discus" by sculptor George Baker was specifically designed for the library and added to an interior staircase in November 1973.[34]

- Construction of a $11 million alumni center began in May 2008. The center is expected to be opened in fall 2009 and house the SDSU Alumni Association, the Campanile Foundation, as well as the university relations and development staff.[35]

Residence halls

In 1937, Quetzal Hall, the first dormitory, opened for 40 women students and was located off campus.[25] In 1952, 50 college youth conducted a panty raid at Quetzal Hall, causing $1,000 in damages. Police arrested 13 of the students and the dorm girls later retaliated by attacking the Pi Kappa Alpha fraternity house.[36] In 1968, the coed dorm Zura Hall was built, and more rooms were added later.[37] Chapultepec Hall held 580 students when first built.[38]

Branch campuses

* Imperial Valley Campus
  * Located in Calexico, California
  * Additional campus in Brawley, California along with research park and related facilities
  * Upper division, teacher certification, and graduate classes only
* North County Campus
  * Formerly located in northern San Diego County
  * Closed; converted to California State University, San Marcos
* South Bay Campus
  * Formerly located on the first floor of the parking structure across from the Holiday Inn in National City, California.
  * Shared facilities with Southwestern College.
  * Closed indefinitely.

Academics

Fall Freshman Statistics[39] [40] [39]

	2011	2010	2009	2008	2007
Applicants	45,027	44,845	41,986	50,148	46,718
Admits	14,805	13,447	15,273	15,658	20,628
% Admitted	32.88	29.99	36.38	31.22	44.15

Research affairs

San Diego State University is the leader in the California State University system in awarding Ph.D. (joint with UCSD [41]) or Ed.D degrees, currently awarding such degrees in 16 academic disciplines. As a result of recent statutory changes (SB 724), SDSU intends to expand the scope and number of doctoral degree programs that it offers its graduate students. SDSU has been referred to as the research flagship campus of the California State University system.

Rankings and distinctions

University rankings (overall)	
National	
ARWU[42]	112-137
U.S. News & World Report[43]	164
Washington Monthly[44]	175
Global	
ARWU[45]	301-400

- For four years in a row, SDSU has been ranked the No. 1 most productive research university, among schools with 14 or fewer Ph.D. programs based on the Faculty Scholarly Productivity Index.[10]
- SDSU has been designated a "Research University" with high research activity by the Carnegie Foundation.
- Since 2000, SDSU faculty and staff have attracted more than $1 billion in grants and contracts for research and program administration.
- SDSU is the largest university in San Diego and the fifth largest in California.
- SDSU ranks No. 2 among universities of its type nationwide and No. 1 in California for students studying abroad as part of their college experience.[46]
- One in seven adults in San Diego who holds a college degree attended SDSU.
- SDSU is home to the first-ever MBA program in Global Entrepreneurship. As part of the program, students study at four universities worldwide, including the United States, China, the Middle East, and India. Corporate partners include Qualcomm, Invitrogen, Intel, Microsoft, and KPMG.
- In 1970, SDSU founded the first women's studies program in the country.
- Modern Healthcare ranked SDSU No.2 Graduate school for physician executives in relation to their Master's in Public Health program.[47]

Organization and administration

Schools and colleges

- College of Arts & Letters
- College of Business Administration
- College of Education
- College of Engineering
- College of Health & Human Services (and Graduate School of Public Health)
- College of Sciences
- College of Professional Studies & Fine Arts
- College of Extended Studies (and American Language Institute)

A landmark architecture (Hepner Hall) featured in the school's logo

Endowment

See also San Diego State University Research Foundation for additional information

The permanent financial endowment of San Diego State University (SDSU) is currently valued at $120.3 million U.S. dollars (USD) as of the end of the 2007 academic year.[48]

Pedestrian bridge connecting various residence halls and parking structures to campus

Student Services building with clock tower

The primary philanthropic arm of San Diego State University is The Campanile Foundation [49], controlled by the University Advancement division [50] of the university. The San Diego State University Research Foundation, an auxiliary corporation owned and controlled by the university, is the manager and administrator of all philanthropic funds and external funding for the university and its affiliated and auxiliary foundations and corporations.

As of June 30, 2006, permanent assets of the SDSU Campanile Foundation totaled $134 million.[51]

For the 2004-2005 academic year, SDSU received over $157 million USD in external funding from grants and contracts, as well as an additional $57 million USD in donations and charitable giving.[52] For 2005-2006, SDSU received $152 million USD in grants and contracts to support research. This is followed by $47.7 million USD in donations, gifts and other charitable giving.[53]

An auxiliary to The Campanile Foundation is the Aztec Athletic Association [54], which primarily raises funds for the student athletes in the San Diego State University athletics programs (see discussion of Athletics below and at SDSU Aztecs).

In addition to its permanent endowment, San Diego State University raises over $55 million U.S. dollars per year (approximately) in philanthropic gifts to support its research and academic affairs.[55]

The California State University system budget is being cut by $564 million this year, with SDSU's budget being reduced by $55 million.[56] As a result of California's state budget cuts, student enrollment is being reduced by 4,618 by Fall 2010.[57]

Media, newspapers, and magazines

Students began publishing *The White and Gold* in 1902, which was a literary magazine and newspaper.[58] In 1913, a new newspaper was established entitled *Normal News Weekly*.[59] The school newspaper *Paper Lantern* (*Normal News Weekly* was renamed after the addition of the junior college) became *The Aztec* in September 1925.[60] It was later expanded to its current name, *The Daily Aztec*. The school's annual yearbook was named *Del Sudoeste* (Spanish for "of the southwest") in the early 1920s. *The Koala*, a comedy newspaper that is widely known around the San Diego State area, is also distributed monthly on campus but is not directly connected to the school at the moment.[60]

Malcolm A. Love Library and the InfoDome

SDSU media and publications

- San Diego State University Press
  - The oldest university press in the California State University system with noted specializations in Border Studies, Critical Theory, Latin American Studies, and Cultural Studies.
- Hyperbole Books
  - Hyperbole Books
- KPBS Public Broadcasting TV/FM
  - Television, digital television, and FM radio for the San Diego community
  - Official site of KPBS
  - An affiliate of the Public Broadcasting Service (PBS) network
  - "A Broadcasting Service of San Diego State University"
- KCR (AM)
  - Student-run broadcast station
- 360 Magazine
  - The quarterly SDSU alumni and San Diego community magazine

Official SDSU campus newspapers

- The SDSU News & Media webpage
- SDSUniverse news service
  - News and information for the SDSU community
- The Daily Aztec - The largest daily collegiate newspaper in California, publishing daily since 1960.

Extracurriculars

Athletics

The first major sport on campus was rowing, but it initially had no coaches or tournaments.[61] Other sports that developed early in the campus's history were tennis, basketball, golf, croquet, and baseball.[61] The school's football program had such a limited selection of players that faculty had to be used to fill the roster.[61] When the college merged with the junior college in 1921, SDSU became a member of the Junior College Conference. After the school won the majority of the conference titles in a variety of sports, the league requested that SDSU leave out of fairness to the smaller schools. For its football program, the team outscored its opponents 249 to 52 in ten games, resulting in the first sales of season tickets in 1923.[62] From 1925-26, SDSU played as an independent. It then joined the Southern California Conference in 1926, where it did not win a football conference championship until 1936. However, in other sports including tennis and basketball, it excelled.[62] SDSU remained with the conference until 1939, when it joined the California Collegiate Athletic Association.[63]

The basketball team reached and won multiple championships games during the 1930-1940s, including a conference title in 1931, 1934, 1937, and 1939. It reached the national championship in 1939 and 1940, losing in the final rounds. However, in 1941 SDSU returned and won the college's first national title.[63] In track, the team won conference titles in 1935, 1936, 1937, 1938, and 1939.[63] The football team won conference titles in 1936 and 1937, and the baseball team won three conference titles and placed second three times between 1935-1941.[63]

In 1955, the Aztec Club was established and raised $20,000 a year by 1957. The club worked in increasing athletic scholarships, hiring better coaches, and developing the college's intercollegiate athletic programs. In 1956, students approved through a vote of allowing a mandatory student activity fee, with a portion going to athletics. By the end of the decade the budget had doubled to $40,000. The campus's most successful sports program during the 1950s was cross-country as the team won eight straight conference titles, AAU regional titles, and placed high in national competitions. Basketball ranged from last in the conference to multiple conference, regional, and national appearances. The football program had its first undefeated team in 1951, but in the last part of the decade earned the worst records in the school's football program under the direction of head coach Paul Governali.[64]

Under Governali, the campus's football program suffered, due to Governali's policy of not recruiting new players. To improve the program, Love hired Don Coryell in 1961, which helped the program to win three consecutive championships (1966–68), and end with a record of 104 wins, 19 losses, and 2 ties by the time he left SDSU. Coryell was assisted by John Madden, Joe Gibbs, and Rod Dowhower, among others. In Coryell's first year, attendance at home games averaged 8,000 people, but by 1966 it had doubled to 16,000. This later jumped to 26,000-41,000 per game with the addition of the new San Diego stadium. At some games, attendance was larger than at San Diego Chargers games. There were several undefeated seasons and multiple players broke records for most catches, touchdowns, and

Marshall Faulk's game ball from the September 14, 1991 game when he ran for a NCAA-record 386 yards and scored 44 points

passing yards, among others. In 1969, SDSU moved into NCAA Division 1, leaving the California Collegiate Athletic Association. In 1972, Coyrell left to pursue coaching in the NFL.[65]

Basketball also did well, with the 1967-68 team being ranked the number one college-level team in the nation, although it did not win a national title. The Aztecs also won the 1960 CCAA baseball title, and won multiple national championships throughout the 1960s in track, cross country, and swimming.[65]

By 1970-71, the campus had 14 NCAA sports. The 1973 men's volleyball team won the NCAA national championship which was the first NCAA national title since moving to Division I status.[66]

SDSU competes in NCAA Division I FBS. Its primary conference is the Mountain West Conference; its women's water polo team participates in the Mountain Pacific Sports Federation and its men's soccer team participates as an Associate Member of the Pacific-12 Conference (the "Pac-12" Conference). The ice hockey team competes in the ACHA with other western region club teams (www.sdsuhockey.com). The crew team's championship regatta is in the WIRA (Western International Rowing Association). The university colors are scarlet (red) and black, SDSU's athletic teams are nicknamed "Aztecs", and its current mascot is the Aztec Warrior, historically referred to as "Monty - Montezuma". Athletics revenues have been down recently.[67]

Football

See San Diego State Aztecs football

- The football team plays at Qualcomm Stadium (formerly known as "Jack Murphy" Stadium).

Basketball

See San Diego State Aztecs men's basketball

- The basketball teams play at Viejas Arena on the SDSU campus.

Baseball

- The baseball team plays in Tony Gwynn Stadium on the SDSU campus, named after the SDSU baseball and basketball player and current head coach, Tony Gwynn.

Viejas Arena is used for the Aztec basketball games, speeches, convocations, and concerts

Volleyball

- The women's volleyball team plays in Peterson Gym on the SDSU campus.
- The men's volleyball team won the NCAA Championship in 1973, but the team has since been disbanded.

Soccer

- Both the men's and women's teams both play at the Sports Deck on the SDSU campus. The women compete in the Mountain West Conference while the men compete in the Pacific-12 Conference (Pac-12).

Ice Hockey

- Participates in the ACHA Men's Division 2.
- Advanced to National Championship final game in 2008 for ACHA Men's Division 3 and lost 7-3 to California University of Pennsylvania.
- San Diego State University Ice Hockey

Other sports

- The new $12 million dollar aquatic sports complex (known as the Aztec Aquaplex), includes an Olympic-size swimming pool, a separate recreational pool and beach, and a hydrotherapy spa. This facility is home for the swimming and diving teams, in addition to providing recreational use for all SDSU students and community members.
  - SDSU Campus Recreation pool web page
- In conjunction with the UCSD, the Associated Students organization of San Diego State University runs the Mission Bay Aquatic Center (MBAC) in Mission Bay, California, just a few miles west of the main campus. The MBAC provides for all manner of outdoor activities and sports for SDSU students, administration, and faculty.

Clubs

Initial clubs that were first started on campus including the Debating Club, the Associated Student Body, YWCA, and in 1906, an alumni association.[58] The oldest club on campus was The Rowing Association.[68]

Student body and Greek life

The underground San Diego Trolley station on the SDSU campus

The first fraternity on campus was the Delta chapter of Epsilon Eta, which formed on October 25, 1921. By the end of the decade there were six other fraternities and eight sororities. The fraternities and sororities were all local, and did not attain national status until after World War II.[68] In 1925, in order to encourage higher grades, the Inter-Fraternity Council and Inter-Sorority Council published the average grades of the fraternity and sorority members. On a 3.0 scale, the average GPA (grade point average) for all students was 1.49, for fraternities was 1.35, and sororities was 1.47.[68] By the mid-1930s there were eight fraternities and eleven sororities,[25] and later expanded to fifteen fraternities and twelve sororities in the 1940s.[69] The first fraternity to go national was Theta Chi and the first sorority was Alpha Xi Delta.[69]

On April 27, 1974, the Phi Beta Kappa honor society established a SDSU chapter. It was the first in the CSU system as well as the San Diego area.[70] During the 1960s and early 1970s, the Greek population had dwindled to 699, but gradually began to increase in the 1980s, reaching 2,900 in 1988. There were 20 fraternities and 13 sororities officially affiliated with the Inter Fraternity Council and Panhellenic Council as well as six independent fraternities/sororities. This made it one of the largest fraternity and sorority systems in the western U.S.[71] On April 6, 1978, Gamma Phi Beta sorority hired a plane to drop marshmallows on fraternity houses during Derby Week, but the plane crashed near Peterson Gym, injuring four students aboard.[72] In 1983 a *USA Today* article reported that SDSU Greeks GPAs were below the campus average, so SDSU tightened restrictions and supervision and by 1989 their grades had increased to slightly above University average.[72] Between 1989-91, several riots among the fraternities occurred, including one numbering 3,500 people, and another requiring 34 police officers to end it.[73] The 2008 drug bust resulted in the suspension of several fraternities as well as the arrests of multiple fraternity members.[74] Currently there are over 48 social fraternities and sororities, including both general and culturally based organizations, represented by four governing councils.

Traditions

- The San Diego State Marching Aztecs and Pep and Varsity Bands are often seen at many sporting events including Football, Basketball and even Volleyball.
- The San Diego State University (SDSU) campus is known as "Montezuma Mesa", as the university is situated on a mesa overlooking Mission Valley and is located at the intersection of Montezuma Road and College Avenue.
- Undie Run through campus that takes place during finals week each semester.

Courtyard looking towards Hepner Hall

S mountain

"S" mountain was created by the Council of Twelve and initially supported by President Hardy. On February 27, 1931, he allowed 500 students to paint rocks, forming a 400-foot "S" on Cowles Mountain. The giant S was lit at night for the opening football game of a season (performed by the freshman to build school spirit) along with pep rallies, and was repainted throughout its history.[75] [22] At the time, it was the largest collegiate symbol in the world.[76] During World War II, the S was camouflaged to prevent it becoming a reference point for enemy bombing aircraft.[77] It was returned to its normal state in April 1944.[78] In the 1970s students stopped painting it and brush obstructed the symbol. After a 1988 brush fire it was exposed, and students repainted it. In fall, 1997, a group of 100 volunteers climbed Cowles Mountain after dusk to commemorate the one hundredth anniversary of the school by using flashlights to once again outline the "S" on the side of the mountain. In 1990, a high school prank defaced the S to read as "91" in honor of their graduating class.[79]

School colors and mascot

The initial colors of the school were white and gold. When the junior college was added to the campus in 1921, its colors of blue and gold were merged together, resulting in a blue, gold, and white color scheme. New colors were later chosen as gold and purple, until being replaced by crimson and black on January 28, 1928.[80]

The school's prior nicknames for its mascot included "Normalites", "Professors", and "Wampus Cats". However, after a 1924 committee met to address the issue, the name "Aztecs" was decided on.[60] In 2003, the Aztec Warrior was approved by a student and alumni vote to become the official university mascot after the school's prior mascot, Monty Montezuma, was discontinued.[81]

Notable events and popular culture

Film and television

- The two main characters from the 2004 Academy Award-winning comedy/drama film *Sideways* were roommates during their college days at SDSU.
- The SDSU campus is the setting of Hearst College, the fictional university in The CW television network show *Veronica Mars*.
- The exterior shots of Rancho Carne High School in the movie *Bring it On* were mainly filmed at San Diego State University
- Portions of *The Real World: San Diego* were filmed around the SDSU campus

- SDSU is mentioned by Bart Simpson in *The Simpsons* episode "The President Wore Pearls" (Season 15, 2003). Lisa becomes president of Springfield Elementary and unknowingly strips the school of all of its recreational activities, leading Bart to say, "Lisa, you made this school even worse. And it wasn't exactly San Diego State to begin with."

1996 campus shooting

The San Diego State University shooting occurred on August 15, 1996. A 36-year-old graduate engineering student, while apparently defending his thesis, shot and killed his three professors, Constantinos Lyrintzis, Cheng Liang, and D. Preston Lowrey III, at San Diego State University. The shooter, who was suffering from certain mental problems, was convicted on July 19, 1997, and was sentenced to life in prison. As a memorial, tables with a plaque with information about each victim have been placed adjacent to the College of Engineering building.

2008 student drug arrests

On May 6, 2008, the Drug Enforcement Administration announced the arrest of 96 individuals, of whom 33 were San Diego State University students, on a variety of drug charges in a narcotics sting operation dubbed Operation Sudden Fall.[82] It was originally reported that 75 of the arrested were students, but the inflated number included students who had been arrested months earlier, in some cases for simple possession.[83] The bust, which was the largest in the history of San Diego County, drew a mixed reaction from the community.[84] In addition, Associated Students President, James Poet was arrested on October 17, 2008, for driving under the influence and possession of marijuana. Poet expressed full support for the actions of Operation Sudden Fall and the Zero Tolerance Policy. [85]

References

[1] "Recession hits colleges' endowments" (http://www.nacubo.org/Documents/research/ 2010NCSE_Public_Tables_Endowment_Market_Values_Final.pdf). NACUBO. . Retrieved February 8, 2011.

[2] "San Diego State University" (http://collegesearch.collegeboard.com/search/CollegeDetail.jsp?match=true&collegeId=951& searchType=college&type=qfs&word=San Diego State University). collegeboard.com. .

[3] http://www.sdsu.edu

[4] http://www.thedailyaztec.com/2011/04/with-low-acceptance-rates-sdsu-enters-new-chapter

[5] http://www.cbs8.com/story/14258884/sdsu-announces-13k-applicants-accepted-for-fall-semester?clienttype=printable

[6] Carnegie Foundation: San Diego State University (http://www.carnegiefoundation.org/classifications/sub.asp?key=748& subkey=13612&start=782)

[7] Study Ranks California's Most Productive Universities (May 31, 2007) (http://www.prweb.com/releases/2007/5/prweb529904.htm)

[8] SDSU named most productive small research school (North County Times) (June 1, 2007) (http://www.nctimes.com/articles/2007/06/ 02/news/sandiego/14_57_336_1_07.txt)

[9] SDSU Receives Top Research Distinction for Second Straight Year (SDSUniverse.com) (Nov. 26, 2007) (http://www.sdsuniverse.info/ story.asp?id=61084)

[10] SDSU is No.1 in Rankings (July 19, 2010) (http://www.thedailyaztec.com/campus-news/sdsu-is-no-1-in-rankings-1.2280576)

[11] "Tech's 29 Most Powerful Colleges" (http://www.thedailybeast.com/galleries/1578/21/?redirectURL=http://www.thedailybeast.com/ blogs-and-stories/2010-05-03/techs-29-most-powerful-colleges/#gallery=1578;page=21). The Daily Beast. .

[12] SDSU Significant Rankings and Distinctions (http://advancement.sdsu.edu/marcomm/news/sdsufacts.html)

[13] "San Diego State University" (http://www.carnegiefoundation.org/classifications/sub.asp?key=748&subkey=13612&start=782) (database entry and article). carnegiefoundation.org. .

[14] Robbins, Gary (14 May 2010). "Funds for research are flowing into SDSU" (http://www.signonsandiego.com/news/2010/may/14/ funds-for-research-are-flowing-into-sdsu/). San Diego, California: San Diego Union-Tribune. pp. A1. .

[15] Mount Laguna Observatory

[16] Forty Years Later, the Magic of JFK Lingers on the Mesa (http://sdsuniverse.info/story.asp?id=6269), Coleen L. Geraghty, *SDSUniverse* (May 12, 2003)

[17] *SDSU Library*, Aztec Bowl: History of San Diego State University (accessed Jan. 16, 2009) (http://infodome.sdsu.edu/projects/ buildings/aztecbowl.html)

[18] John F. Kennedy commencement address (June 6, 1963), SDSU Special Collections (video) (http://scua.sdsu.edu/exhibits/online/2010/ 03/JFKMovie/JFKMovie.shtml)

[19] Diego State University, Library & Information Access, "President John F. Kennedy's 1963 Commencement Speech at San Diego State (video and audio archive) (http://library.sdsu.edu/scua/exhibits-and-events/online-exhibits/kennedy|San)

[20] http://library.sdsu.edu/scua/exhibits-and-events/online-exhibits/kennedy

[21] "Historic Buildings of San Diego State University" (http://dometest.sdsu.edu/projects/buildings/bldgs.html). *Infodome - SDSU Historic Buildings*. San Diego State University. . Retrieved 2009-07-30.

[22] Starr, p. 78

[23] Starr, p. 156

[24] Starr, p. 94

[25] Starr, p. 96

[26] Starr, p. 191

[27] Starr, p. 202

[28] "Hardy Memorial Tower" (http://dometest.sdsu.edu/projects/buildings/hardy.html). *Infodome - SDSU Historic Buildings*. San Diego State University. . Retrieved 2009-07-30.

[29] Starr, p. 125

[30] Starr, p. 138

[31] Starr, p. 155-56

[32] Starr, p. 187

[33] Starr, p. 188

[34] Starr, p. 189

[35] Lee, Jaimy (2008-04-14). "Tucker Sadler has designs on $11m center at SDSU" (http://www.accessmylibrary.com/coms2/summary_0286-34442995_ITM). San Diego Business Journal. . Retrieved 2008-10-11.

[36] Starr, p. 143

[37] Starr, p. 168

[38] Starr, p. 220

[39] (http://university-stats.sdsu.edu/app/reports/Glance/glance.pdf). *SDSU Profile, Fall 2011*.

[40] (http://www.calstate.edu/as/stat_reports/2010-2011/apps_fall10.shtml). *CSU Analytic Studies, Fall 2010*.

[41] San Diego State University's Academic Programs (http://www.sdsu.edu/academicprogs.html)

[42] "Academic Ranking of World Universities: National" (http://www.shanghairanking.com/ARWU2011.html). Institute of Higher Education, Shanghai Jiao Tong University. 2011. . Retrieved August 30, 2011.

[43] "National Universities Rankings" (http://colleges.usnews.rankingsandreviews.com/best-colleges). *America's Best Colleges 2012*. U.S. News & World Report. September 13, 2011. . Retrieved September 25, 2011.

[44] "The Washington Monthly National University Rankings" (http://www.washingtonmonthly.com/college_guide/rankings_2011/national_university_rank.php). *The Washington Monthly*. 2011. . Retrieved August 30, 2011.

[45] "Academic Ranking of World Universities: Global" (http://www.shanghairanking.com/ARWU2011.html). Institute of Higher Education, Shanghai Jiao Tong University. 2011. . Retrieved August 30, 2011.

[46] "San Diego State University | The Impact of the California State University" (http://www.calstate.edu/impact/campus/sandiego.html). Calstate.edu. . Retrieved 2010-09-12.

[47] "SDSU No. 2 Grad School for Physician Execs" (http://newscenter.sdsu.edu/sdsu_newscenter/news.aspx?s=72190). *newscenter.sdsu.edu*. . Retrieved 12 September 2010.

[48] "Raising the fundraising bar" San Diego Union Tribune, February 12, 2008 (http://www.signonsandiego.com/uniontrib/20080212/news_1n12funds.html)

[49] http://newscenter.sdsu.edu/tcf/

[50] http://advancement.sdsu.edu/index.html

[51] The Campanile Foundation: Financial Statements June 30, 2006 (http://advancement.sdsu.edu/tcf/download/Campanile_05-06 final.pdf)

[52] 2004-2005 Annual Report on External Funding, California State University (http://www.calstate.edu/UA/0405externalreport/campus/san_diego.shtml)

[53] 2005-2006 Annual Report on External Support to the CSU -- San Diego State University (http://www.calstate.edu/ua/0506externalreport/campus/san_diego.shtml)

[54] http://goaztecs.collegesports.com/boosters/boosters-static-info/booster-overview.html

[55] "San Diego State University Reports $55.2 Million in Philanthropic Gifts for 2004-05" Official SDSU Press Release, Oct. 7, 2005" (http://advancement.sdsu.edu/marcomm/news/releases/fall2005/pr100705b.html)

[56] Ruggero, Lorena. " Aztecs Rally Against Budget Cuts (http://www.palomar.edu/dsps/actc/mla/mlainternet.html)". October 9, 2009.

[57] Weber, Stephen. " SDSU Admissions Changes (http://advancement.sdsu.edu/budgetcentral/index.html)". San Diego State University. October 21, 2009.

[58] Starr, p. 27

[59] Starr, p. 39

[60] Starr, p. 53

[61] Starr, p. 28

[62] Starr, p. 60

[63] Starr, p. 102 & 105

[64] Starr, p. 144-45

[65] Starr, p. 159-62

[66] Starr, p. 221

[67] Schrotenboer, Brent (February 22, 2008). "Football shy of dollar goal at SDSU" (http://www.signonsandiego.com/uniontrib/20080222/news_1s22azbudget.html). *San Diego Union-Tribune*. . Retrieved 2008-02-25

[68] Starr, p. 59

[69] Starr, p. 127

[70] Starr, p. 193

[71] Starr, p. 214

[72] Starr, p. 215

[73] Starr, p. 216

[74] McDonald, Jeff; Sherry Saavedra and Tanya Sierra (2008-05-07). "Major SDSU drug probe nets 96 arrests in raids" (http://www.signonsandiego.com/news/metro/20080507-9999-1n7drugs.html). San Diego Union Tribune. . Retrieved 2008-11-04.

[75] Starr, p. 126

[76] Starr, p. 79

[77] Starr, p. 112

[78] Starr, p. 121

[79] Starr, p. 213

[80] Starr, p. 50

[81] Jenkins, Brandon; Melissa Berlant (2003-12-15). "San Diego State U.: San Diego State U. approves university mascot" (http://www.accessmylibrary.com/coms2/summary_0286-19718715_ITM). The America's Intelligence Wire. . Retrieved 2008-11-10.

[82] "Mug Shots from Operation Sudden Fall" (http://web.archive.org/web/20080530031254/http://www.cbs8.com/misc/SDSU_mug_shots.pdf) (PDF). CBS News 8. Archived from the original (http://www.cbs8.com/misc/SDSU_mug_shots.pdf) on 2008-05-30. . Retrieved 2008-05-06.

[83] "Officials differ on number of SDSU students snared in sting" (http://www.signonsandiego.com/news/metro/20080508-1041-bn08arrests.html). San Diego Union Tribune. . Retrieved 2008-05-08.

[84] "SDSU drug sting draws scorn, praise" (http://www.signonsandiego.com/news/metro/20080508-9999-1n8sdsu.html). San Diego Union Tribune. . Retrieved 2008-05-08.

[85] "Poet arrested for alleged DUI and marijuana possession" (http://www.thedailyaztec.com/city/poet_arrested_for_alleged_dui_and_marijuana_possession). The Daily Aztec. . Retrieved 2008-10-25.

External links

- Official website (http://http://www.sdsu.edu)
- Official athletics website (http://www.goaztecs.com/)

University_of_Illinois_at_Urbana–Champaign

University of Illinois at Urbana–Champaign	
Motto	Learning and Labor
Established	1867
Type	Flagship, land-grant, sea-grant, space-grant, public university
Endowment	US$ 955.6 million[1]
Chancellor	Phyllis Wise[2]
President	Michael Hogan[3]
Provost	Robert Easter (interim)[4]
Academic staff	2,971
Admin. staff	8,085
Students	41,495
Undergraduates	31,173
Postgraduates	10,322
Location	Urbana and Champaign, Illinois, United States
Campus	Micro-urban **unknown operator: u','** acres (**unknown operator: u','ha**)
Former names	Illinois Industrial University (1867–1885) University of Illinois (1885–1982)
Athletics	NCAA Division I-FBS, 21 varsity teams (10 men's, 11 women's)
Colors	Illinois Blue[5] Illinois Orange[5]
Nickname	Fighting Illini
Affiliations	Big Ten Conference Committee on Institutional Cooperation
Website	http://illinois.edu/

The **University of Illinois at Urbana–Champaign** (**U of I**, **UIUC**, or simply **Illinois**) is a large public research-intensive university in the state of Illinois, United States. It is the flagship campus of the University of Illinois system. The University of Illinois at Urbana–Champaign is the second oldest public university in the state, second to Illinois State University, and is a founding member of the Big Ten Conference. It is considered a Public Ivy and is a member of the Association of American Universities. The university is designated as a RU/VH Research University (very high research activities).[6] The campus library system possesses the third-largest university library in the United States and the sixth-largest in the country overall.[7]

The university comprises 17 colleges that offer more than 150 programs of study. Additionally, the university operates an extension[8] that serves 2.7 million registrants per year around the state of Illinois and beyond. The campus holds 286 buildings on **unknown operator: u','** acres (**unknown operator: u','**ha) in the twin cities of Champaign and Urbana; its annual operating budget in 2011 was over $1.7 billion.[9]

History

The Morrill Act of 1862 granted each state in the United States a portion of land on which to establish a major public state university, one which could teach agriculture, mechanic arts, and military training, "without excluding other scientific and classical studies."[10] This phrase would engender controversy over the University's initial academic philosophies, polarizing the relationship between the people of Illinois and the University's first president, John Milton Gregory.[11]

After a fierce bidding war between a number of Illinois cities, Urbana was selected in 1867 as the site for the new school.[10] From the beginning, Gregory's desire to establish an institution firmly grounded in the liberal arts tradition was at odds with many State residents and lawmakers who wanted the university to offer classes based solely around "industrial education"[12] The University finally opened for classes on March 2, 1868, with only two faculty members and a small group of students. The debate between the liberal arts curriculum and industrial education continued in the University's inaugural address, as

John Milton Gregory

Dr. Newton Bateman outlined the various interpretations of the Morrill Act in his speech.[13] Gregory's thirteen year tenure would be marred by this debate. Clashes between Gregory and legislators and lawmakers forced his resignation from his post as president in 1880, saying "[I am] staggering under too heavy a load of cares, and irritated by what has sometimes seemed as needless opposition."[11] Today, Gregory is largely credited with establishing the University and forming it into the major interdisciplinary university it is today. Gregory's grave is still located on the Urbana campus, situated between Altgeld Hall and the Henry Administration Building. His marker (mimicking the epitaph of British architect Christopher Wren) reads, "If you seek his monument, look about you."

The university experienced rapid growth following World War II under president David Henry, under whom the university doubled enrollment and significantly improved its academic standing.[14] This period was also marked by large growth in the Graduate College and increased federal support of scientific and technological research. The state of Illinois supplied roughly two-thirds of the university's budget while the federal government funded 90% of research.[15] In recent years, state support has declined from 4.5% of the state's tax appropriations in 1980 to 2.28% in 2011, a nearly 50% decline.[16] As a result, the university's budget has strongly shifted away from relying on state support with nearly 84% of the budget now coming from other sources.[17]

Evolution of name

The original proposed name in 1867 was "Illinois Industrial University." In 1885, the Illinois Industrial University officially changed its name to the University of Illinois, reflecting its holistic agricultural, mechanical, and liberal arts curricula.[12] This remained the official name for nearly 100 years, until it was changed to The University of Illinois at Urbana–Champaign in 1982, ostensibly to establish a separate identity for the campus within the University of Illinois system. However, after a century's use, UIUC continues to be known and referred to as "The University of Illinois", or just "Illinois"; this is true in both the media,[18] [19] and on many of UIUC's web pages.[20] [21] [22] Starting in 2008, the university began strongly rebranding itself as "Illinois" rather than UIUC, changing the website URL from uiuc.edu to Illinois.edu as well as all email addresses.

Colleges and schools

UIUC offers study through 16 colleges. Advanced undergraduate students may participate in a rigorous course of study through the *James Scholar Honors Program* and earn highest distinctions with University Honors.

- College of Agriculture, Consumer, and Environmental Sciences
- College of Applied Health Sciences
- Institute of Aviation
- College of Business
- College of Education
- College of Engineering
- College of Fine and Applied Arts
- Graduate College
- School of Labor and Employment Relations
- College of Law
- College of Liberal Arts and Sciences
- Graduate School of Library and Information Science
- College of Media
- College of Medicine at Urbana–Champaign
- School of Social Work
- College of Veterinary Medicine

Campus

The campus is known for its landscape and architecture, as well as distinctive landmarks.[23] It was identified as one of 50 college or university 'works of art' by T.A. Gaines in his book *The Campus as a Work of Art*.[24]

The main research and academic facilities are divided almost exactly between the twin cities of Urbana and Champaign. The College of Agriculture, Consumer, and Environmental Sciences' research fields stretch south from Urbana and Champaign into Savoy and Champaign County. The university maintains formal gardens and a conference center in nearby Monticello at Allerton Park.

U of I is one of the few educational institutions to own an airport.[25] Willard Airport, named for former University of Illinois president Arthur Cutts Willard, is located in Savoy. It was

Foellinger Auditorium

completed in 1945 and began service in 1954. Willard Airport is home to University research projects and the University's Institute of Aviation, along with flights from American Airlines.

The campus is based on the quadrangle design popular at many universities. Four main quads compose the center of the university and are arranged from north to south. The Beckman Quadrangle and the John Bardeen Quadrangle occupy the center of the Engineering Campus. Boneyard Creek flows through the John Bardeen Quadrangle, paralleling Green Street. The Beckman Quadrangle is primarily composed of research units and laboratories, and features a large solar calendar consisting of an obelisk and several copper fountains. The Main Quadrangle and South Quadrangle follow immediately after the John Bardeen Quad. The former makes up a large part of the Liberal Arts and Sciences portion of the campus, while the latter comprises many of the buildings of the College of ACES spread across the campus map.[26]

Sustainability

In October, 2010, the Sustainable Endowments Institute gave the campus a grade of B for sustainability in its 2011 College Sustainability Report Card. Strengths noted in the report included the campus's adoption of LEED gold standards for all new construction and major renovations and its public accessibility to endowment investment information. The university makes a list of endowment holdings and its shareholder voting record available to the public. The weaknesses comprise of areas such as student involvement and investment priorities. The student sustainability committee is empowered to allocate funding from a clean energy technology fee and a sustainable campus environment fee, while the university aims to optimize investment return but has not made any public statements about investigating or investing in renewable energy funds or community development loan funds. However the biggest weakness of the university's sustainability is its shareholder engagement, as the university has not made any public statements about active ownership or a proxy voting policy.[27]

In his remarks on the creation of the Office of Sustainability in September, 2008, Chancellor Richard Herman stated, "I want this institution to be the leader in sustainability."[28] In February, 2008, he signed the American College and University Presidents Climate Commitment, committing the University of Illinois to take steps "in pursuit of climate neutrality."

Research

Having been classified into the category comprehensive doctoral with medical/veterinary and very high research activity,[29] by The Carnegie Foundation for the Advancement of Teaching, Illinois offers a wide range of disciplines in undergraduate and postgraduate programs. It is also listed as one of the Top 25 American Research Universities by The Center for Measuring University Performance.[30] Beside annual influx of grants and sponsored projects, the university manages an extensive modern research infrastructure.[31] The university has been a leader in computer based education and hosted the PLATO project, which was a precursor to the internet and resulted in the development of the plasma display.

The university hosts the National Center for Supercomputing Applications (NCSA), which created Mosaic, the first graphical Web browser, the foundation upon which Mozilla Firefox and Microsoft Internet Explorer are based, the Apache HTTP server, and NCSA Telnet. The Parallel@Illinois program hosts several programs in parallel computing, including the Universal Parallel Computing Research Center. The university is currently collaborating with IBM and the National Science Foundation to build the world's fastest supercomputer.[32] This supercomputer, named "Blue Waters," aims to be capable of performing one quadrillion calculations per second. If completed, this would make Blue Waters three times faster than today's fastest supercomputer. The university whimsically celebrated January 12, 1997 as the "birthday" of HAL 9000, the fictional supercomputer from the novel and film *2001: A Space Odyssey*; in both works, HAL credits "Urbana, Illinois" as his place of operational origin.

In 1952, the university built the ILLIAC (Illinois Automatic Computer), the first computer built and owned entirely by an educational institution. U of I is also the site of the Department of Energy's Center for the Simulation of

Advanced Rockets, an institute which has employed graduate and faculty researchers in the physical sciences and mathematics. It performs materials science and condensed matter physics research, and is home to Frederick Seitz Materials Research Laboratory as well as the Micro and Nanotechnology Laboratory. Two complexes for research and teaching recently opened, Siebel Center for Computer Science in 2004 and the Institute for Genomic Biology in 2006. The Beckman Institute for Advanced Science and Technology, however, is still the largest interdisciplinary facility on campus with 313000 square feet (29100 m^2). Both the Illinois Natural History Survey and Illinois State Geological Survey are located on campus and affiliated with the university. The university also conducts agricultural and horticultural research.

Since 1957 the Illinois Transportation Archaeological Research Program (ITARP [33]) has conducted archaeological and historical compliance work for the Illinois Department of Transportation. ITARP serves as a repository for a large collection of Illinois archaeological artifacts now numbering over 17,000 boxes. One of the major collections is from the Cahokia Mounds,[34] for which ITARP has over 550 boxes. An on-line database will soon be mounted for the Cahokia collection, funded by a 2008–2010 National Endowment for the Humanities grant.

In the 24 February 2004 talk as part of his Five Campus Tour (Harvard, MIT, Cornell, Carnegie-Mellon and Illinois),[35] titled "Software Breakthroughs: Solving the Toughest Problems in Computer Science," Bill Gates has mentioned that Microsoft hires more graduates from the University of Illinois than from any other university in the world.[36] Alumnus William M. Holt, a Senior Vice-President of Intel, also mentioned in a campus talk in 27 September 2007 entitled "R&D to Deliver Practical Results: Extending Moore's Law"[37] that Intel hires more PhD graduates from the University of Illinois than from any other university in the country.

In 2007, the university-hosted research Institute for Condensed Matter Theory (ICMT) was launched, with the director Paul Goldbart and the chief scientist Anthony Leggett. ICMT is currently located at the Engineering Science Building on campus.

Student life

Competition

According to the statistics of the 2008 admitted freshmen, 77% of incoming students had ACT score of 27 or higher, 31% had an SAT combined Math & Critical Reading score above 1,400 (excludes Writing), and 59% of the incoming students were top 10% of their high school class.[38] Some of the university's colleges admit students at an even more competitive level. For incoming freshmen in 2008, the College of Engineering reported an ACT score interquartile range of 30–33, the College of Business reported an ACT score IQR of 28–32, and the College of Media, in 2008, the first year it accepted freshmen, reported an ACT IQR of 27–32, higher than the overall campus median (though still lower than that of the College of Engineering). Of graduates, Illinois ended up as one of the top 12 (percentage) and top 6 (numerical) feeder state colleges to elite professional schools.[39]

Residences

University Residence Halls and University Private-Certified Housing are administered by the University's housing division.[40] University housing for undergraduates is provided through twenty-two residence halls in both Urbana and Champaign.

All undergraduates within the University housing system are required to purchase some level of meal plan, although they are free to eat elsewhere if they choose. Graduate housing is usually offered through two graduate dormitories, restricted to those over twenty years of age, and through two university-owned apartment complexes. However, the recent record-sized freshman class has forced the housing division to convert one of the graduate dormitories into undergraduate housing. Students with disabilities are provided special housing options to accommodate their needs.

There are a number of private dormitories around campus, as well as a few houses that are outside of the Greek system and offer a more communal living experience. The private dorms tend to be more expensive to live in compared to other housing options. Private, certified residences maintain reciprocity agreements with the University, allowing students to move between the public and private housing systems if they are dissatisfied with their living conditions.

Most undergraduates choose to move into apartments or the Greek houses after their first or second year. The University Tenant Union offers advice on choosing apartments and the process of signing a lease.

Greek life

The university has the largest Greek system in the world by membership.[41] There are currently sixty-eight fraternities and thirty-six sororities on the campus. Of the approximately 31,180 undergraduates,[42] about 3,330 are members of sororities[43] and about 3,370 are members of fraternities. The Greek system at the University of Illinois has a system of self-government. While there are staff advisors and directors in charge of managing certain aspects of the Greek community, most of the day to day operations of the Greek community are governed by the Interfraternity Council and Panhellenic Council.[44] Many of the fraternity and sorority houses on campus are on the National Register of Historic Places.

Business Fraternities

There are four business fraternities at the university. The largest and oldest, Alpha Kappa Psi, was installed at the university in 1913. The Epsilon [45] chapter of Alpha Kappa Psi was the fifth chapter chartered in the United States after its first incorporation at New York University in 1904. As of 2011, the Epsilon chapter is only one of eight chapters internationally to receive membership awards.[46] Notable alumni from the Epsilon [47] chapter include former Illinois Senator Paul Douglas, Governor Otto Kerner, U.S. Steel President Leslie Worthington. Other business fraternities at the university include Delta Sigma Pi (Upsilon), Phi Chi Theta (Zeta Gamma) and Phi Gamma Nu (Beta Pi chapter).

Student Government

The current university student government, created in 2005, is the Illinois Student Senate, a combined undergraduate and graduate student senate with 54 voting members. The student senators are elected by college and represent the students on a variety of faculty and administrative committees, and are led by an internally elected executive board consisting of a President, External Vice-President, Internal Vice-President, and a treasurer.

Libraries

The campus library system is one of the largest public academic collections in the world.[48] Among universities in North America, only the collections of Harvard and Yale are larger.[49] Currently, the University of Illinois' main library and 40 other departmental libraries and divisions hold more than 22 million items, including more than 12 million volumes.[50] As of 2006, it had also the largest "browsable" university library in the United States, with 7.5 million volumes directly accessible in stacks in a single location. UIUC also has the largest public engineering library (Grainger Engineering Library) in the country.[51]

The online catalog is used by over one million people monthly. In addition to the main library building, which houses nearly 20 subject-oriented libraries, the Isaac Funk Family Library on the South Quad serves the College of Agriculture, Consumer, and Environmental Sciences and the Grainger Engineering Library Information Center serves the College of Engineering on the John Bardeen Quad.

The University of Illinois Residence Hall Library System[52] is one of three in the nation.[53] The Residence Hall Libraries were created in 1948 to serve the educational, recreational, and cultural information needs of first and second year undergraduate students residing in the residence halls, and the living-learning communities within the residence halls. The collection also serves University Housing staff as well as the larger campus community, including undergraduate and graduate students, and university faculty and staff.[54]

All together there are more than 40 departmental or school libraries on campus.

Recreation

The Urbana–Champaign campus has a modern recreation infrastructure.[55] Recently, the two main recreation facilities, CRCE and the Activities and Recreation Center (ARC, formerly known as IMPE), were upgraded.[56] The campus also has more than a thousand clubs and organizations, ranging from cultural and athletic to subject area to philanthropic. Students can create their own Registered Student Organization if the pursuing interest/concern is not addressed by the current entities.[57]

Transportation

The bus system that operates throughout the campus and community is operated by the Champaign-Urbana Mass Transit District. The MTD receives a student-approved transportation fee from the university, which provides unlimited access for university students. In addition, the university pays for universal access for all its faculty and staff. As part of this arrangement, the MTD also runs a bus line between Willard Airport and Illinois Terminal, a multi-modal transportation facility which includes Amtrak and Greyhound – making it the focal point of Champaign-Urbana's public transportation systems.

The university maintains an extensive system of off-street bike paths and on-street bike lanes on campus. All students are expected to register their bicycles with the campus public safety department.

Athletics and sports

U of I's Division of Intercollegiate Athletics fields teams for ten men's and eleven women's varsity sports. The university participates in the NCAA's Division 1. The university's athletic teams are known as the Fighting Illini. The university operates a number of athletic facilities, including Memorial Stadium for football, the Assembly Hall for men's and women's basketball, and the Atkins Tennis Center for men's and women's tennis. The men's NCAA basketball team had a dream run in the 2005 season, with Bruce Weber's Fighting Illini tying the record for most victories in a season. Their run ended 37–2 with a loss to the North Carolina Tar Heels in the national championship game.

Illinois is a member of the Big Ten Conference.

On October 15, 1910, the Illinois football team defeated the University of Chicago Maroons with a score of 3–0 in a game that Illinois claims was the first homecoming game, though several other schools claim to have held the first homecoming as well.[58] [59]

On November 10, 2007, the unranked Illinois football team defeated the #1 ranked Ohio State football team in Ohio Stadium, the first time that the Illini beat a #1 ranked team on the road.

The University of Illinois Ice Arena is home to the university's club college ice hockey team competing at the ACHA Division I level and is also available for recreational use through the Division of Campus Recreation. It was built in 1931 and designed by Chicago architecture firm Holabird and Root, the same firm that designed the University of Illinois Memorial Stadium and Chicago's Soldier Field. It is located on Armory Drive across from the Armory. The structure features 4 rows of bleacher seating in an elevated balcony that runs the length of the ice rink on either side. These bleachers provide seating for roughly 1,200 fans, with standing room and bench seating available underneath. Because of this set-up the team benches are actually directly underneath the stands.[60]

Chief Illiniwek, or 'The Chief', was the university's official athletic symbol from 1926 until February 21, 2007. Use of the Chief garnered criticism for the university starting in the mid-1970s from Native Americans and others as a misappropriation and inaccurate portrayal of indigenous culture. The university officials announced the end of the Chief Illiniwek era on February 16, 2007.

Notable among a number of songs commonly played and sung at various events such as commencement and convocation, and athletic games are: Illinois Loyalty, the school song, Oskee Wow Wow, the fight song, and Hail to the Orange, the alma mater, which was based on "Sammy,"a song from Williston Northampton School, a prep School in Easthampton, Massachusetts.

Academic awards and recognition

University Honors

University Honors is an academic distinction awarded to high achieving students at UIUC. It is comparable to the Latin honors of summa cum laude. Graduating students awarded *University Honors* must have a cumulative grade point average of a 3.5/4.0 within the academic year of their graduation and rank within the top 3% of their graduating class.[61]

James Scholars

"James Scholars" are undergraduate students invited to pursue a specialized course of study for no less than two years of their undergraduate course work. Each student must have a minimum grade point average of 3.3/4.0 (3.5 for ECE majors) to become a James Scholar. James Scholars who graduate with "University Honors" are also awarded the Latin honors of In cursu honorum.[62]

Chancellor's Scholars

"Chancellor's Scholars" is a campus scholarship program which focuses on both academic excellence and leadership. Unlike the James Scholars Program, the Campus Honors Program may only have about 125 members at any given time. Chancellor's scholars must have a grade point average of 3.3/4.0, successfully complete a total of five CHP sponsored courses, and participate in a specified number of CHP co-curricular events and activities.[63]

Senior 100 Honorary

"Senior 100 Honorary" is an award from the Student Alumni Ambassadors and the University of Illinois Alumni Association that recognizes outstanding seniors. Recipients of this award are honored for their outstanding achievements in leadership, academics and campus involvement throughout their undergraduate education.[64]

Notable faculty and alumni

Alma Mater

As of 2007, 21 alumni and faculty members are Nobel laureates and 20 have won a Pulitzer Prize.[41] In particular, John Bardeen is the only person to have won two Nobel prizes in physics, having done so in 1956 and 1972 while on faculty at the University of Illinois. In 2003, two faculty members won Nobel prizes in different disciplines: Paul C. Lauterbur for physiology or medicine, and Anthony Leggett for physics. Most recently, in 2007, Don Wuebbles, Atul Jain, John Walsh and Michael Schlesinger, professors in the Department of Atmospheric Science, were awarded a share of the Nobel Peace Prize for their contributions and collaboration with the IPCC.[65]

Stanley Hart White, Professor of Landscape Architecture 1922-1959. Inventor of the Vertical Garden. E.B White's Brother

Fazlur Rahman Khan, considered to be the *Einstein of structural engineering* and the *Greatest Structural Engineer of the of the 20th Century*[66]

Alumni have created companies and products such as Netscape Communications, AMD, PayPal, Playboy, National Football League, Siebel Systems, Mortal Kombat, CDW, YouTube, THX, Oracle, Lotus, Mosaic, Safari, Firefox, W. W. Grainger, Delta Air Lines, BET, and Tesla Motors.

Alumni and faculty have invented the LED, JavaScript, the integrated circuit, the quantum well laser, the transistor, MRI, and the plasma screen, and are responsible for the structural design of such buildings as the Willis Tower, the John Hancock Center, and the Burj Khalifa.[67]

Alumni founded the Susan G. Komen for the Cure, the Rainbow/PUSH Coalition, Project Gutenberg, and have served in a wide variety of government and public interest roles.

Rafael Correa, re-elected President of The Republic of Ecuador in April 2009 secured his M.S. and Ph.D degrees from the University's Economics Department in 1999 and 2001 respectively.[68]

Nathan C. Ricker attended U of I and in 1873 was the first person to graduate in the United States with a degree in Architecture. Mary L. Page, the first woman to obtain a degree in architecture, also graduated from U of I.[69]

Philanthropy

Philanthropy is playing an increasingly significant role in supporting the Land Grant mission of the University of Illinois. The portion of the university's annual $1.5 billion budget which is state funds has diminished drastically over the past two decades. Currently the university receives only 16.4% of its budget from state tax dollars compared to 20 years ago when it received 44.5% of its budget from state tax dollars.[70] Gifts, grants, and contracts to the university comprise 19% of the annual budget.

Philanthropic giving to the university comes in the form of annual giving, major gifts, and estate planning. Annual giving is generally unrestricted by the donor and can be spent by the campus to meet immediate needs to maintain basic operations. Major gifts are typically put into an endowment at the donor's wishes, where the principal of the gift is invested while the interest is distributed to the campus department in which the donor designated their gift to be used. This practice of investing the principal in an endowment and only spending the interest, is done to secure the gift in perpetuity. In some cases, major gifts are used immediately for building campaigns such as the Krannert Center for the Performing Arts, The Beckman Institute, or The Thomas M. Siebel Center for Computer Science. Estate planning is another type of giving whereby a donor makes provisions in their will or estate documents which identifies the University of Illinois as a beneficiary.

Alumni play the largest role in philanthropic giving to the university. The most notable donors are Thomas M. Siebel and his wife Stacey who recently gave a $100 million estate gift to the university after they had given $36 million to build the Thomas M. Siebel Center for Computer Science, $10 million to endow the Siebel Scholars program, $2 million to endow the Thomas M. Siebel Chair in Computer Science and $2 million to endow the Thomas M. Siebel Chair in the History of Science. Other notable donors include Sohaib Abbasi and his wife, Sara, who established the Sohaib and Sara Abbasi Professorship to enable the CS department to maintain its stature as one of the nation's premiere departments and give students the opportunity to learn from a world-renowned computer scientist and educator. They have also endowed the Sohaib and Sara Abbasi Fellowship to allow up to 5 graduate students each year, the opportunity to study computer science at one of the nation's top ranked computer science departments.

Stanley O. and Judith L. Ikenberry were the 14th President and First Lady of the Urbana-Champaign campus of the University of Illinois from 1979–1995. The Ikenberrys established the Stanley O. and Judith L. Ikenberry Endowment for Krannert Center for the Performing Arts. This gift supports the presentation of guest artists at the Center as part of the Marquee Endowment.

Rankings

University rankings (overall)	
National	
ARWU[71]	19
Forbes[72]	147
U.S. News & World Report[73]	45
Washington Monthly[74]	38
Global	
ARWU[75]	25
QS[76]	61
Times[77]	31

In its 2012 listings, *U.S. News & World Report* ranked the undergraduate program 45th among nationally accredited universities and 13th among nationally accredited public universities.[78] The graduate program had 60 disciplines ranked within the top 30 nationwide, including 23 within the top five. U.S. News & World Report ranked the undergraduate and graduate Accounting programs 2nd and 4th respectively in the United States in their 2011 rankings; both programs had been ranked 1st at the same time in previous years. The College of Business as a whole was ranked 12th nationally. The College of Engineering was ranked 5th at the graduate level, with 14 disciplines ranked within the top ten. Chemistry and Physics were also ranked within the top ten at the graduate level. The College of Education had six programs ranked within the top ten. The Graduate School of Library and Information Science was ranked 1st, with five programs ranked within the top ten. Many arts programs were ranked within the first quartile, such as Architecture and Fine Arts. However, Computer Science, Material Science, Agricultural Engineering, Civil Engineering, Electrical Engineering, Mechanical Engineering, Accounting, Finance, and Psychology are the university's most visibly distinguished departments among others. The School of Labor and Employment Relations is ranked consistently within the top two in the nation, behind only Cornell University.

The University of Illinois is considered a "Public Ivy" and is measured comprehensively as one of the top 20 major research universities in the United States by a Graham-Diamond Report.[79]

International rankings by The Institute of Higher Education at Shanghai Jiao Tong University suggest that Illinois is the 19th best university in North America, and 25th best university in the world.[80] The Academic Ranking of World Universities by Broad Subject Fields from the same research center in 2008 positions Illinois in 3rd for Engineering/Technology and Computer Sciences in the world. It is ranked 19th for Life and Agriculture Sciences, 20th for Natural Sciences and Mathematics, and 51st for Social Sciences.[81]

In 2011, Illinois was ranked 61st in the world by QS World University Rankings,[82] increasing its position from the 2009 THE-QS World University Rankings (in 2010, Times Higher Education World University Rankings and QS World University Rankings parted ways to produce separate rankings). However, Illinois had been ranked within the top 40 in the past. The THE-QS rankings have been criticized due to their volatility: it stressed international popularity and ranks fluctuated tens of places from one year to the next.[83] The WSJ ranking of business schools also has this inherited anomaly, attributable to its survey method.

The Institute for Labor and Industrial Relations has been recognized consistently as one of the top three programs for Human Resources and Labor Relations studies in the United States[84].

In the 2008 release of Webometrics Ranking of World Universities by Cybermetrics Lab, which is a research unit of the National Research Council of Spain, the University was ranked 9th.[85] In 2006, G-Factor, another academic list trying to measure social network efficacy of universities, has ranked Illinois within the top eight.[86] A human competitiveness index and analysis by the Human Resources & Labor Review, and published in Chasecareer Network, ranked the university 25th internationally in 2010.[87] As of 2007, Washington Monthly ranks Illinois as the 11th best university in the nation, and 9th among public universities. The methodology of the ranking includes "how well it performs as an engine of social mobility," "how well it does in fostering scientific and humanistic research," and "how well it promotes an ethic of service to country."[88]

Newsweek International listed Illinois as one of Top 100 Global Universities,[89] which "takes into account openness and diversity, as well as distinction in research." Kiplinger's Personal Finance also listed Illinois in its 100 Best Values in Public Colleges,[90] which "measures academic quality, cost and financial aid."

The Princeton Review has elected Illinois one of the 366 best colleges out of nearly 5,000 degree-granting institutions of higher education in the United States.[91] Nonetheless, the university has come under criticism for its use of graduate teaching assistants in teaching undergraduate courses, including upper-level undergraduate courses. For two consecutive years, the Urbana–Champaign campus topped this review's[92] category of "teaching assistants teach too many upper level courses." However, the Princeton Review's ranking has been scrutinized for its lack of accountability as the Review's ranking categorical data rely mainly upon student random sampling.

Controversies

2005-2009 century admissions scandal

A series of investigative reports by the *Chicago Tribune* noted that between 2005 and 2009 university trustees, president, chancellor, and other administrators pressured admissions officials into admitting under-qualified but politically well-connected applicants into the university.[93] [94] Although University officials initially denied,[95] then downplayed the existence of a "clout list",[96] the university later announced it would form a panel of internal and external representatives to review the past admissions process and determine possible changes.[97] The *Chicago Tribune* took the University to court for summary judgment, which was granted [98] in March 2011. The University appealed, and a number of organizations, including the Electronic Privacy Information Center [99], filed "friend of the court" briefs [100] on behalf of both parties.

Howell firing

In July 2010 The News-Gazette reported[101] that Dr. Kenneth Howell, an adjunct professor teaching Introduction to Catholic Thought, was fired for teaching the Roman Catholic positions on homosexuality. The Alliance Defense Fund has taken up Dr. Howell's case, stating that his dismissal is a violation of academic freedom and the First Amendment. The University's position, as stated by Ann Mester, associate dean of the College of Arts and Sciences, is that Dr. Howell's comments "violate university standards of inclusivity, which would then entitle us to have him discontinue his teaching arrangement with us."

Dr. Howell was reinstated by the University of Illinois as an adjunct instructor for the fall 2010 term to teach "Introduction to Catholicism", resolving the situation for the time being.[102] The university announced on July 28 that it would follow the recommendation of the Academic Senate's General University Policy Committee to begin paying the salary of instructors teaching Catholic studies courses. St. John's Catholic Newman Center previously paid instructor salaries. The matter is currently under review by the Academic Senate Committee on Academic Freedom and Tenure.[103]

See also

- List of University of Illinois at Urbana–Champaign people - List of notable University of Illinois People
- Daily Illini – independent student newspaper
- WPGU – student-run commercial radio station
- Illinois Loyalty – school song
- Fighting Illini – University of Illinois at Urbana–Champaign sports
- Marching Illini – marching band of the University of Illinois at Urbana–Champaign

References

[1] http://premium.usnews.com/best-colleges/university-of-illinois-urbana-champaign-1775

[2] Office of the Chancellor Homepage (http://oc.illinois.edu)

[3] Fain, Paul (13 May 2010), "How Michael Hogan Landed in Illinois" (http://chronicle.com/article/How-Michael-Hogan-Landed-in/65544/
), *Chronicle of Higher Education*, Leadership & Governance, , retrieved 22 August 2010

[4] Board of Trustees Agenda, November 12, 2009 (http://www.uillinois.edu/trustees/agenda/November 12, 2009/002a nov Interim
Provost-Chancellor.pdf)

[5] http://identitystandards.illinois.edu/graphicstandardsmanual/generalguidelines/colors.html

[6] [Carnegie Foundation for the Advancement of Teaching. http://www.carnegiefoundation.org/classifications/sub.asp?key=748&
subkey=16731&start=782."University of Illinois at Urbana-Champaign"]. Carnegie Foundation for the Advancement of Teaching. .

[7] American Library Association, " ALA Library Fact Sheet 22 – The Nation's Largest Libraries: A Listing by Volumes Held (http://www.ala.
org/ala/professionalresources/libfactsheets/alalibraryfactsheet22.cfm)". July 2010.

[8] "What we do" (http://web.extension.uiuc.edu/state/whatwedo.html). .

[9] "Budget Summary For Operations Fiscal Year 2011" (http://www.obfs.uillinois.edu/common/pages/DisplayFile.aspx?itemId=954470),
University of Illinois, 23 September 2010, pp. 9 (of 131),

[10] Illini Years: A Picture History of the University of Illinois (1950). p.6"

[11] Illini Years: A Picture History of the University of Illinois (1950). p.11"

[12] Brichford, Maynard. (1983), *A Brief History of the University of Illinois* (http://web.library.uiuc.edu/ahx/UIHISTORY.PDF)

[13] "Address of Dr. Newton Bateman" in "Some Founding Papers of the University of Illinois" (Urbana, 1967). p.17

[14] "David D. Henry, 89, President Of Illinois U. in Time of Tumult" (http://www.nytimes.com/1995/09/07/obituaries/
david-d-henry-89-president-of-illinois-u-in-time-of-tumult.html). *The New York Times*. September 7, 1995. .

[15] "A Brief History of the University of Illinois" (http://www.library.illinois.edu/archives/features/history.php). . Retrieved May 26,
2011.

[16] "University of Illinois FY2010 Budget Request" (http://www.pb.uillinois.edu/Documents/budgetbook/FY2012Budgetbook.pdf). .
Retrieved May 26, 2011.

[17] Budget by Source of Funds | Stewarding Excellence @ Illinois (http://oc.illinois.edu/budget/budgetchart1.html)

[18] "University of Illinois to Be Investigated for Politically Connected Acceptances" (http://thechoice.blogs.nytimes.com/2009/06/10/
university-of-illinois-to-be-investigated-for-politically-connected-acceptances/). *The New York Times*. June 10, 2009. .

[19] Cohen, Jodi S (August 18, 2010). "U. of I. opens state-of-the-art dorm for students with disabilities" (http://articles.chicagotribune.com/
2010-08-18/news/ct-met-u-of-i-disability-dorm-20100818_1_dorm-disabilities-students-shower). *Chicago Tribune*. .

[20] http://illinois.edu/about/admin/admin.html

[21] http://illinois.edu/about/community/community.html

[22] http://news.illinois.edu/

[23] "Campus Landmarks" (http://web.archive.org/web/20070819052401/http://www.publicaffairs.uiuc.edu/facts/landmarks.html).
Archived from the original (http://www.publicaffairs.uiuc.edu/facts/landmarks.html) on August 19, 2007. . Retrieved August 30, 2007.

[24] Shari L. Ellertson. "Expenditures on O&M at America's Most Beautiful Campuses" (http://www.appa.org/facilitiesmanager/article.
cfm?ItemNumber=394&parentid=203). APPA. . Retrieved 2007-07-24.

[25] Committee on Campus Operations. UIUC Senate (http://www.senate.uiuc.edu/co0402.asp). April 26, 2004.

[26] "" (http://web.archive.org/web/20051107045227/http://www.uiuc.edu/images/maps/campusmap.gif). Archived from the original
(http://www.uiuc.edu/images/maps/campusmap.gif) on November 7, 2005. . Retrieved November 23, 2005.

[27] "University of Illinois" (http://www.greenreportcard.org/report-card-2011/schools/university-of-illinois). . Retrieved December 9, 2011.

[28] "Chancellor directs trustees' attention to faculty salaries" (http://media.www.dailyillini.com/media/storage/paper736/news/2008/09/
11/News/Updated.Chancellor.Directs.Trustees.Attention.To.Faculty.Salaries-3426224.shtml). . Retrieved October 15, 2008.

[29] Carnegie Classifications (http://www.carnegiefoundation.org/classifications/sub.asp?key=748&subkey=14086&start=782)

[30] Research- The Center for Measuring University Performance (http://mup.asu.edu/research.html)

[31] About Us: Buildings and Facilities – ECE ILLINOIS | University of Illinois at Urbana-Champaign (http://www.ece.uiuc.edu/about/
buildings.html)

[32] "National Science Board Approves Funds for Petascale Computing Systems" (http://www.nsf.gov/news/news_summ. jsp?cntn_id=109850&org=OCI&from=news). . Retrieved 2007-08-24.

[33] http://www.itarp.uiuc.edu/

[34] http://www.cahokiamounds.com/cahokia.html

[35] http://www.microsoft.com/presspass/exec/billg/speeches/2004/02-24UnivIllinois.aspx

[36] News & Events I Department of Computer Science at Illinois (http://www.cs.uiuc.edu/news/articles.php?id=2004Feb27-1)

[37] Computer Science Department Calendar (http://webtools.uiuc.edu/calendar/Calendar?ACTION=VIEW_EVENT&calId=504& skinId=47&DATE=9/27/2007&eventId=71363)

[38] "Student Selectivity" (http://www.oar.uiuc.edu/future/apply/requirements_freshman.html). . Retrieved December 30, 2008.

[39] The Wall Street Journal Classroom Edition (http://www.wsjclassroomedition.com/college/feederschools.htm)

[40] "Housing Home" (http://www.housing.uiuc.edu). . Retrieved November 23, 2005.

[41] "Facts 2008: Illinois by the numbers" (http://www.publicaffairs.uiuc.edu/facts/facts.html). UIUC Public Affairs. . Retrieved June 22, 2008.

[42] "University of Illinois system enrolls 70,195 on three campuses" (http://www.uillinois.edu/our/news/2008/sep11.enrollment.cfm). . Retrieved September 22, 2008.

[43] "Fraternity and Sorority Affairs" (http://www.odos.uiuc.edu/GREEK/scholarship/panGrades.asp). . Retrieved September 22, 2008.

[44] "" (http://web.archive.org/web/20051224213203/http://www.odos.uiuc.edu/greek/IFCchapterMembership.xls). Archived from the original (http://www.odos.uiuc.edu/greek/IFCchapterMembership.xls) on December 24, 2005. . Retrieved April 24, 2006.

[45] http://www.business.illinois.edu/akpsi

[46] http://en.wikipedia.org/wiki/Chapters_of_Alpha_Kappa_Psi

[47] http://business.illinois.edu/akpsi

[48] http://www.publicaffairs.uiuc.edu/facts/facts.html

[49] http://www.arl.org/bm~doc/arlstat08.pdf

[50] "Rankings" (http://web.archive.org/web/20060826152850/http://www.ala.org/ala/alalibrary/libraryfactsheet/alalibraryfactsheet22. htm). Archived from the original (http://www.ala.org/ala/alalibrary/libraryfactsheet/alalibraryfactsheet22.htm) on August 26, 2006. . Retrieved September 3, 2006.

[51] http://publicaffairs.illinois.edu/rankings/

[52] Living-Learning Communities I University Housing at Illinois (http://www.housing.uiuc.edu/living/library/)

[53] "Residence Hall Libraries" (http://www.housing.uiuc.edu/living/library/). .

[54] "About Us" (http://www.housing.uiuc.edu/living/library/aboutus.htm). .

[55] http://www.campusrec.uiuc.edu/

[56] Campus Recreation » University of Illinois (http://www.campusrec.uiuc.edu/)

[57] U of I Admissions: Get Involved (http://www.oar.uiuc.edu/future/campuslife/organizations/index.html)

[58] "Columbia Missourian — Tradition's beginnings mysterious" (http://columbiamissourian.com/sports/story.php?ID=22348). .

[59] "Origin of the University Homecoming" (http://www.admin.uiuc.edu/homecoming/history.pdf) (PDF). . Retrieved December 13, 2005.

[60] Staff (July 26, 2006). "Ice Arena Facility" (http://web.archive.org/web/20060426003535/http://www.campusrec.uiuc.edu/facilities/ ice_arena.html). University of Illinois, Division of Campus Recreation. Archived from the original (http://www.campusrec.uiuc.edu/ facilities/ice_arena.html) on 2006-04-26. . Retrieved 2006-08-22.

[61] University Honors – the Bronze Tablets (http://images.library.uiuc.edu/projects/bronze/)

[62] James Scholar Honors Program, The Division of General Studies, University of Illinois (http://www.dgs.Illinois.edu/honors/ jamesscholar.html)

[63] U of I Admissions: Campus Honors Program (http://admissions.Illinois.edu/academics/honors_campus.html/)

[64] (http://www.uiaa.org/illinois/honors/senior100.html)

[65] List of All Nobel Laureates 2007 (http://nobelprize.org/nobel_prizes/lists/2007.html)

[66] Ali Mir (2001), *Art of the Skyscraper: the Genius of Fazlur Khan*, Rizzoli International Publications, ISBN 0-8478-2370-9

[67] www.SOM.com I William F. Baker (http://www.som.com/content.cfm/william_f_baker)

[68] Markey, Patrick. Ecuador's Correa leaps from outsider to take lead (http://www.washingtonpost.com/wp-dyn/content/article/2006/10/ 11/AR2006101101081.html), *Washington Post*, 11 October 2006

[69] Professor Paul Kruty. Establishing Architecture at the University of Illinois (http://www.arch.uiuc.edu/about/history/ricker/). Last updated May 28, 2005.

[70] Budget by Source of Funds I Stewarding Excellence @ Illinois (http://oc.illinois.edu/budget/budgetchart1.html)

[71] "Academic Ranking of World Universities: National" (http://www.shanghairanking.com/ARWU2011.html). Institute of Higher Education, Shanghai Jiao Tong University. 2011. . Retrieved August 30, 2011.

[72] "America's Best Colleges" (http://www.forbes.com/top-colleges/list/). Forbes. 2011. . Retrieved October 6, 2011.

[73] "National Universities Rankings" (http://colleges.usnews.rankingsandreviews.com/best-colleges). *America's Best Colleges 2012*. U.S. News & World Report. September 13, 2011. . Retrieved September 25, 2011.

[74] "The Washington Monthly National University Rankings" (http://www.washingtonmonthly.com/college_guide/rankings_2011/ national_university_rank.php). *The Washington Monthly*. 2011. . Retrieved August 30, 2011.

[75] "Academic Ranking of World Universities: Global" (http://www.shanghairanking.com/ARWU2011.html). Institute of Higher Education, Shanghai Jiao Tong University. 2011. . Retrieved August 30, 2011.

[76] "QS World University Rankings" (http://www.topuniversities.com/university-rankings/world-university-rankings/2011). QS Quacquarelli Symonds Limited. 2011. . Retrieved September 30, 2011.

[77] "Top 400 – The Times Higher Education World University Rankings 2011–2012" (http://www.timeshighereducation.co.uk/world-university-rankings/2011-2012/top-400.html). The Times Higher Education. 2011. . Retrieved October 6, 2011.

[78] "America's Best Colleges 2009" (http://colleges.usnews.rankingsandreviews.com/college/national-search). U.S. News & World Report. 2007. . Retrieved 2009-10-01.

[79] http://www.physics.northwestern.edu/graduate/Graham_Diamond.html

[80] "Academic Ranking of World Universities 2007" (http://ed.sjtu.edu.cn/rank/2007/ARWU2007_Top100.htm). Institute of Higher Education, Shanghai Jiao Tong University. 2007-07-31. . Retrieved 2007-11-20.

[81] "Academic Rankings of World Universities by Broad Subject Fields – 2007" (http://ed.sjtu.edu.cn/ARWU-FIELD.htm). Institute of Higher Education, Shanghai Jiao Tong University. 2007-01-31. . Retrieved 2007-11-20.

[82] http://www.topuniversities.com/university-rankings/world-university-rankings/2011?page=1

[83] Holmes, Richard. "The THES University Rankings: Are They Really World Class?" (http://web.archive.org/web/20071127115614/http://www.geocities.com/universities06/ajueart.pdf) (PDF). *Asian Journal of University Education (volume 1, issue 1).* Geocities.com. Archived from the original (http://web.archive.org/web/20110511211908/http://www.geocities.com/universities06/ajueart.pdf) on 2007-11-27. . Retrieved 2007-11-20. *Note: Existence of the journal has not been verified as of November 2007*

[84] "ILIR : About the Institute, University of Illinois" (http://www.ilir.uiuc.edu/aboutilir/index.htm). .

[85] "Premier League" (http://web.archive.org/web/20071115014623/http://www.webometrics.info/premierleague.asp). *World Universities' ranking on the Web.* Cybermetrics Lab, *Centro Superior de Investigaciones Científicas.* January 2007. Archived from the original (http://www.webometrics.info/premierleague.asp) on 2007-11-15. . Retrieved 2007-11-20.

[86] Peter Hirst (2006). "Top 20 Universities 2006" (http://www.universitymetrics.com/tiki-index.php?page=Top+20+Universities+2006). *Global University Rankings.* University Metrics.com. . Retrieved 2007-11-20.

[87] :: Chase & Associates :: (http://www.chasecareer.net/news_detail.php?id=61)

[88] Nick Baumann; David Freedlander, Oliver Haydock, and Zachary Roth (2007-09-08). "College Rankings" (http://www.washingtonmonthly.com/features/2007/0709.natlrankings.pdf) (PDF). *National Universities. The Washington Monthly.* . Retrieved 2007-11-20.

[89] http://www.msnbc.msn.com/id/14321230/site/newsweek/

[90] Rankings for 100 Best Values in Public Colleges – Kiplinger (http://www.kiplinger.com/tools/colleges/)

[91] Degree-granting institutions and branches, by type and control of institution and state or jurisdiction: 2005–06 (http://nces.ed.gov/programs/digest/d06/tables/dt06_249.asp)

[92] "University tops one list on Princeton Review" (http://media.www.dailyillini.com/media/storage/paper736/news/2004/08/24/News/University.Tops.One.List.On.Princeton.Review-704496.shtml). Daily Illini. August 24, 2004. . Retrieved May 23, 2007.

[93] Cohen, Jodi; St. Clair, Stacy; Malone, Tara (May 29, 2009). "Clout goes to college" (http://www.chicagotribune.com/news/local/chi-college-clout-29-may29,0,84289,print.story). Chicago Tribune. .

[94] "University of Illinois admits it bowed to clout on admissions" (http://www.chicagotribune.com/news/local/chi-college_clout_satmay30,0,1301917.story). Chicago Tribune. May 30, 2009. .

[95] White denies Tribune's corruption reports; student trustee: some "will need to go down" | The Daily Illini (http://www.dailyillini.com/news/campus/2009/05/29/white-denies-tribunes-corruption-reports-student-trustee-some-will-need-to-go)

[96] "U of I chief says 'he'll correct admissions policy" (http://www.chicagobreakingnews.com/2009/05/u-of-i-chief-says-clout-list-had-little-impact.html). Chicago Tribune. May 29, 2009. .

[97] St. Clair, Stacy; Cohen, Jodi S.. "Clout goes to college: clout list put on suspension" (http://www.chicagotribune.com/news/local/chi-college-clout-02-jun02,0,7886322.story). Chicago Tribune. .

[98] http://epic.org/amicus/tribune/20110311_170232_ferpa_case.pdf

[99] http://epic.org

[100] http://epic.org/amicus/tribune/EPIC_brief_Chi_Trib_final.pdf

[101] "Instructor of Catholicism at UI claims loss of job violates academic freedom" (http://www.news-gazette.com/news/university-illinois/2010-07-09/instructor-catholicism-ui-claims-loss-job-violates-academic-free). July 9, 2010. . Retrieved July 13, 2010.

[102] Brachear, Manya A (July 29, 2010). "U. of I. reinstates Catholic professor" (http://articles.chicagotribune.com/2010-07-29/news/ct-met-u-of-i-catholic-professor-073020100729_1_reinstates-academic-freedom-associate-professor). Chicago Tribune. . Retrieved July 30, 2010.

[103] "UI offers to rehire Catholicism prof, ends funding from Newman Center" (http://www.news-gazette.com/news/religion/2010-07-29/ui-offers-rehire-catholicism-prof-ends-funding-newman-center.html). Champaign News-Gazette. July 29, 2010. . Retrieved August 16, 2010.

External links

- Official website (http://www.illinois.edu)
- Official Athletics website (http://www.fightingillini.com/)
- Daily Illini Online (http://www.dailyillini.com/)
- UIHistories Project: History of the University (http://uihistories.ncsa.uiuc.edu/) / UITours Project: Virtual Tour of UIUC Campus (http://uitours.ncsa.uiuc.edu/) / UIPhotos Project: Photo Galleries of Campus (http:// uiphotos.ncsa.uiuc.edu/)

Information

Information in its most restricted technical sense is an ordered sequence of symbols that can be interpreted as a message. Information can be recorded as signs, or transmitted as signals. Information is any kind of event that affects the state of a dynamic system. Conceptually, information is the message (utterance or expression) being conveyed. This concept has numerous other meanings in different contexts. [1] Moreover, the concept of information is closely related to notions of constraint, communication, control, data, form, instruction, knowledge, meaning, mental stimulus, pattern, perception, representation, and especially entropy.

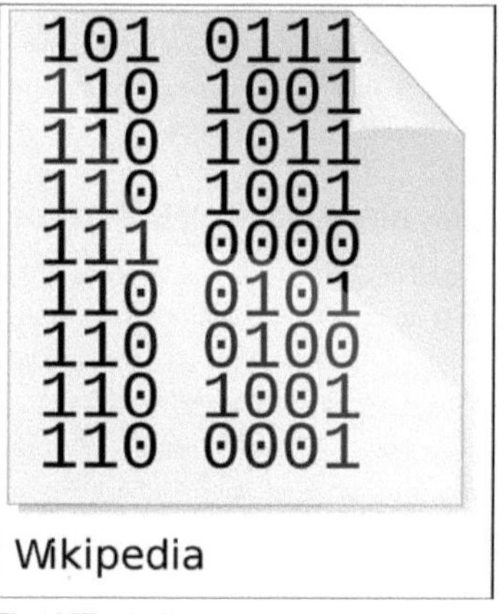

The ASCII codes for the word "Wikipedia" represented in binary, the numeral system most commonly used for encoding computer information.

Etymology

The English word was apparently derived from the Latin stem (*information-*) of the nominative (*informatio*): this noun is in its turn derived from the verb "informare" (to inform) in the sense of "to give form to the mind", "to discipline", "instruct", "teach": "Men so wise should go and inform their kings." (1330) *Inform* itself comes (via French *informer*) from the Latin verb *informare*, to give form, to form an idea of. Furthermore, Latin itself already contained the word *informatio* meaning concept or idea, but the extent to which this may have influenced the development of the word *information* in English is not clear.

The ancient Greek word for *form* was μορφή (*morphe*; cf. morph) and also εἶδος (*eidos*) "kind, idea, shape, set", the latter word was famously used in a technical philosophical sense by Plato (and later Aristotle) to denote the ideal identity or essence of something (see Theory of forms). "Eidos" can also be associated with thought, proposition or even concept.

As sensory input

Often information is viewed as a type of input to an organism or system. Inputs are of two kinds. Some inputs are important to the function of the organism (for example, food) or system (energy) by themselves. In his book *Sensory Ecology,* Dusenbery called these causal inputs. Other inputs (information) are important only because they are associated with causal inputs and can be used to predict the occurrence of a causal input at a later time (and perhaps another place). Some information is important because of association with other information but eventually there must be a connection to a causal input. In practice, information is usually carried by weak stimuli that must be detected by specialized sensory systems and amplified by energy inputs before they can be functional to the organism or system. For example, light is often a causal input to plants but provides information to animals. The colored light reflected from a flower is too weak to do much photosynthetic work but the visual system of the bee detects it and the bee's nervous system uses the information to guide the bee to the flower, where the bee often finds nectar or pollen, which are causal inputs, serving a nutritional function.

As representation and complexity

The cognitive scientist and applied mathematician Ronaldo Vigo argues that information is a relative concept that involves at least two related entities in order to make quantitative sense. These are: any dimensionally-defined category of objects S, and any of its subsets R. R, in essence, is a representation of S, or, in other words, carries or conveys representational (and hence, conceptual) information about S. Vigo then defines the amount of information that R conveys about S as the rate of change in the complexity of S whenever the objects in R are removed from S. Under "Vigo information", pattern, invariance, complexity, representation, and information—five fundamental constructs of universal science—are unified under a novel mathematical framework.[2] Among other things, the framework aims to overcome the limitations of Shannon-Weaver information when attempting to characterize and measure subjective information.

As an influence which leads to a transformation

Information is any type of pattern that influences the formation or transformation of other patterns. In this sense, there is no need for a conscious mind to perceive, much less appreciate, the pattern. Consider, for example, DNA. The sequence of nucleotides is a pattern that influences the formation and development of an organism without any need for a conscious mind.

Systems theory at times seems to refer to information in this sense, assuming information does not necessarily involve any conscious mind, and patterns circulating (due to feedback) in the system can be called information. In other words, it can be said that information in this sense is something potentially perceived as representation, though not created or presented for that purpose. For example, Gregory Bateson defines "information" as a "difference that makes a difference".

If, however, the premise of "influence" implies that information has been perceived by a conscious mind and also interpreted by it, the specific context associated with this interpretation may cause the transformation of the information into knowledge. Complex definitions of both "information" and "knowledge" make such semantic and logical analysis difficult, but the condition of "transformation" is an important point in the study of information as it relates to knowledge, especially in the business discipline of knowledge management. In this practice, tools and processes are used to assist a knowledge worker in performing research and making decisions, including steps such as:

- reviewing information in order to effectively derive value and meaning
- referencing metadata if any is available
- establishing a relevant context, often selecting from many possible contexts
- deriving new knowledge from the information
- making decisions or recommendations from the resulting knowledge.

Stewart (2001) argues that the transformation of information into knowledge is a critical one, lying at the core of value creation and competitive advantage for the modern enterprise.

The Danish Dictionary of Information Terms[3] argues that information only provides an answer to a posed question. Whether the answer provides knowledge depends on the informed person. So a generalized definition of the concept should be: "Information" = An answer to a specific question".

When Marshall McLuhan speaks of media and their effects on human cultures, he refers to the structure of artifacts that in turn shape our behaviors and mindsets. Also, pheromones are often said to be "information" in this sense.

As a property in physics

In 2003, J. D. Bekenstein claimed there is a growing trend in physics to define the physical world as being made of information itself (and thus information is defined in this way) (see Digital physics). Information has a well-defined meaning in physics. Examples of this include the phenomenon of quantum entanglement where particles can interact without reference to their separation or the speed of light. Information itself cannot travel faster than light even if the information is transmitted indirectly. This could lead to the fact that all attempts at physically observing a particle with an "entangled" relationship to another are slowed down, even though the particles are not connected in any other way other than by the information they carry.

Another link is demonstrated by the Maxwell's demon thought experiment. In this experiment, a direct relationship between information and another physical property, entropy, is demonstrated. A consequence is that it is impossible to destroy information without increasing the entropy of a system; in practical terms this often means generating heat. Another, more philosophical outcome is that information could be thought of as interchangeable with energy. Thus, in the study of logic gates, the theoretical lower bound of thermal energy released by an *AND gate* is higher than for the *NOT gate* (because information is destroyed in an *AND gate* and simply converted in a *NOT gate*). Physical information is of particular importance in the theory of quantum computers.

Technologically mediated information

It is estimated that the world's technological capacity to store information grew from 2.6 (optimally compressed) exabytes in 1986, which is the informational equivalent to less than one 730-MB CD-ROM per person in 1986 (539 MB per person), to 295 (optimally compressed) exabytes in 2007.[4] This is the informational equivalent of almost 61 CD-ROM per person in 2007.[5]

The world's combined technological capacity to receive information through one-way broadcast networks was the informational equivalent of 174 newspapers per person per day in 2007.[4]

The world's combined effective capacity to exchange information through two-way telecommunication networks was the informational equivalent of 6 newspapers per person per day in 2007.[5]

As records

Records are a specialized form of information. Essentially, records are information produced consciously or as by-products of business activities or transactions and retained because of their value. Primarily their value is as evidence of the activities of the organization but they may also be retained for their informational value. Sound records management ensures that the integrity of records is preserved for as long as they are required.

The international standard on records management, ISO 15489, defines records as "information created, received, and maintained as evidence and information by an organization or person, in pursuance of legal obligations or in the transaction of business". The International Committee on Archives (ICA) Committee on electronic records defined a record as, "a specific piece of recorded information generated, collected or received in the initiation, conduct or completion of an activity and that comprises sufficient content, context and structure to provide proof or evidence of that activity".

Records may be maintained to retain corporate memory of the organization or to meet legal, fiscal or accountability requirements imposed on the organization. Willis (2005) expressed the view that sound management of business records and information delivered "...six key requirements for good corporate governance...transparency; accountability; due process; compliance; meeting statutory and common law requirements; and security of personal and corporate information."

Information and semiotics

Beynon-Davies[6] [7] explains the multi-faceted concept of information in terms of signs and signal-sign systems. Signs themselves can be considered in terms of four inter-dependent levels, layers or branches of semiotics: pragmatics, semantics, syntax, and empirics. These four layers serve to connect the social world on the one hand with the physical or technical world on the other...

Pragmatics is concerned with the purpose of communication. Pragmatics links the issue of signs with the context within which signs are used. The focus of pragmatics is on the intentions of living agents underlying communicative behaviour. In other words, pragmatics link language to action.

Semantics is concerned with the meaning of a message conveyed in a communicative act. Semantics considers the content of communication. Semantics is the study of the meaning of signs - the association between signs and behaviour. Semantics can be considered as the study of the link between symbols and their referents or concepts; particularly the way in which signs relate to human behaviour.

Syntax is concerned with the formalism used to represent a message. Syntax as an area studies the form of communication in terms of the logic and grammar of sign systems. Syntax is devoted to the study of the form rather than the content of signs and sign-systems.

Empirics is the study of the signals used to carry a message; the physical characteristics of the medium of communication. Empirics is devoted to the study of communication channels and their characteristics, e.g., sound, light, electronic transmission etc..

Nielsen (2008) discusses the relationship between semiotics and information in relation to dictionaries. The concept of lexicographic information costs is introduced and refers to the efforts users of dictionaries need to make in order to, first, find the data sought and, secondly, understand the data so that they can generate information.

Communication normally exists within the context of some social situation. The social situation sets the context for the intentions conveyed (pragmatics) and the form in which communication takes place. In a communicative situation intentions are expressed through messages which comprise collections of inter-related signs taken from a language which is mutually understood by the agents involved in the communication. Mutual understanding implies that agents involved understand the chosen language in terms of its agreed syntax (syntactics) and semantics. The sender codes the message in the language and sends the message as signals along some communication channel (empirics). The chosen communication channel will have inherent properties which determine outcomes such as the speed with which communication can take place and over what distance.

More recently Shu-Kun Lin proposed a simple definition of information: Information is the amount of the data after data compression.

See also

- Abstraction
- Accuracy and precision
- Classified information
- Complexity
  - Complex adaptive system
  - Complex system
- Cybernetics
- Data storage device#Recording medium
- Exformation
- Free Information Infrastructure
- Freedom of information
- Gregory Bateson

- Information and communication technologies
- Information architecture
- Information broker
- Information continuum
- Information entropy
- Information geometry
- Information inequity
- Information infrastructure
- Information ladder
- Information mapping
- Information overload
- Information processing
- Information processor
- Information sensitivity
- Information systems
- Information superhighway
- Information theory
- Infornography
- Infosphere
- Lexicographic information cost
- Library science
- Philosophy of information
- Prediction
- Propaganda model
- Quantum information
- Receiver operating characteristic
- Relevance
- Satisficing
- Shannon–Hartley theorem

References

[1] L. Floridi, Information - A Very Short Introduction (Oxford University Press) (http://ukcatalogue.oup.com/product/9780199551378.
    do?keyword=floridi&sortby=bestMatches) provides a short overview.

[2] Vigo, R. (2011). "Representational information: a new general notion and measure of information". *Information Sciences, 181
    (2011),4847-4859.*.

[3] Informationsordbogen.dk (http://www.informationsordbogen.dk/concept.php?cid=902)

[4] "The World's Technological Capacity to Store, Communicate, and Compute Information" (http://www.sciencemag.org/content/332/6025/
    60), Martin Hilbert and Priscila López (2011), Science (journal), 332(6025), 60-65; free access to the article through here:
    martinhilbert.net/WorldInfoCapacity.html

[5] "video animation on The World's Technological Capacity to Store, Communicate, and Compute Information from 1986 to 2010 (http://
    www.youtube.com/watch?v=iIKPjOuwqHo)

[6] Beynon-Davies P. (2002). Information Systems: an introduction to informatics in Organisations. Palgrave, Basingstoke, UK. ISBN
    0-333-96390-3

[7] Beynon-Davies P. (2009). Business Information Systems. Palgrave, Basingstoke. ISBN 978-0-230-20368-6

Further reading

- Alan Liu (2004). *The Laws of Cool: Knowledge Work and the Culture of Information*, University of Chicago Press
- Bekenstein, Jacob D. (2003, August). Information in the holographic universe. *Scientific American.*
- Gleick, James (2011). The Information: A History, a Theory, a Flood. Pantheon, New York, NY.
- Shu-Kun Lin (2008). 'Gibbs Paradox and the Concepts of Information, Symmetry, Similarity and Their Relationship', *Entropy*, 10 (1), 1-5. Available online at Entropy journal website (http://www.mdpi.com/1099-4300/10/1/1).
- Luciano Floridi, (2005). 'Is Information Meaningful Data?', *Philosophy and Phenomenological Research*, 70 (2), pp. 351 – 370. Available online at PhilSci Archive (http://philsci-archive.pitt.cdu/archive/00002536/01/iimd.pdf)
- Luciano Floridi, (2005). 'Semantic Conceptions of Information', *The Stanford Encyclopedia of Philosophy* (Winter 2005 Edition), Edward N. Zalta (ed.). Available online at Stanford University (http://plato.stanford.edu/entries/information-semantic/)
- Sandro Nielsen: 'The Effect of Lexicographical Information Costs on Dictionary Making and Use', *Lexikos* 18/2008, 170-189.
- Stewart, Thomas, (2001). Wealth of Knowledge. Doubleday, New York, NY, 379 p.
- Young, Paul. The Nature of Information (1987). Greenwood Publishing Group, Westport, Ct. ISBN 0-275-92698-2.

External links

- Semantic Conceptions of Information (http://plato.stanford.edu/entries/information-semantic/) Review by Luciano Floridi for the Stanford Encyclopedia of Philosophy
- Principia Cybernetica entry on negentropy (http://pespmc1.vub.ac.be/ASC/NEGENTROPY.html)
- Fisher Information, a New Paradigm for Science: Introduction, Uncertainty principles, Wave equations, Ideas of Escher, Kant, Plato and Wheeler. (http://www.optics.arizona.edu/Frieden/Fisher_Information.htm) This essay is continually revised in the light of ongoing research.
- How Much Information? 2003 (http://www2.sims.berkeley.edu/research/projects/how-much-info-2003/index.htm) an attempt to estimate how much new information is created each year (study was produced by faculty and students at the School of Information Management and Systems at the University of California at Berkeley)
- (Danish) Informationsordbogen.dk (http://www.informationsordbogen.dk) The Danish Dictionary of Information Terms / Informationsordbogen

xmf:ინფორმაცია rue:Інформація

Data

Data (🔊 /ˈdeɪtə/ *day-tə*, /ˈdætə/ *da-tə*, or /ˈdɑːtə/ *dah-tə*) are qualitative or quantitative attributes of a variable or set of variables. Data are typically the results of measurements and can be the basis of graphs, images, or observations of a set of variables. Data are often viewed as the lowest level of abstraction from which information and then knowledge are derived. *Raw data*, i.e., unprocessed data, refers to a collection of numbers, characters, images or other outputs from devices that collect information to convert physical quantities into symbols.

Physical computer memory elements consists of an addresses and a byte/word of data storage. All data can be reduced to key/value pair combinations. Supersets of this idea, where keys are derived, and values are arranged, relatively, are called data structures. They are also used in peripheral devices.

The word *data* is the plural of *datum*, neuter past participle of the Latin *dare*, "to give", hence "something given". In discussions of problems in geometry, mathematics, engineering, and so on, the terms *givens* and *data* are used interchangeably. Also, data are representations of a fact, figure, and idea. Such usage is the origin of *data* as a concept in computer science: data are numbers, words, images, etc., accepted as they stand.

Usage in English

In English, the word *datum* is still used in the general sense of "an item given". In cartography, geography, nuclear magnetic resonance and technical drawing it is often used to refer to a single specific reference datum from which distances to all other data are measured. Any measurement or result is a *datum*, but *data point* is more usual,[1] albeit tautological. Both *datums* (see usage in datum article) and the originally Latin plural *data* are used as the plural of *datum* in English, but *data* is commonly treated as a mass noun and used with a verb in the singular form, especially in day-to-day usage. For example, *This is all the data from the experiment.* This usage is inconsistent with the rules of Latin grammar and traditional English (*These are all the data from the experiment*). Even when a very small quantity of data is referenced (One number, for example) the phrase *piece of data* is often used, as opposed to *datum*. The debate over appropriate usage is ongoing.

The IEEE Computer Society, allows usage of *data* as either a mass noun or plural based on author preference.[2] Other professional organizations and style guides[3] require that authors treat *data* as a plural noun. For example, the Air Force Flight Test Center specifically states that the word *data* is always plural, never singular.[4]

Data is most often used as a singular mass noun in educated everyday usage.[5] [6] Some major newspapers such as *The New York Times* use it either in the singular or plural. In the *New York Times* the phrases "the survey data are still being analyzed" and "the first year for which data is available" have appeared within one day.[7] In scientific writing *data* is often treated as a plural, as in *These data do not support the conclusions*, but it is also used as a singular mass entity like *information*. British usage now widely accepts treating *data* as singular in standard English,[8] including everyday newspaper usage[9] at least in non-scientific use.[10] UK scientific publishing still prefers treating it as a plural.[11] Some UK university style guides recommend using *data* for both singular and plural use[12] and some recommend treating it only as a singular in connection with computers.[13]

Meaning of data, information and knowledge

The terms data, information and knowledge are frequently used for overlapping concepts. The main difference is in the level of abstraction being considered. Data is the lowest level of abstraction, information is the next level, and finally, knowledge is the highest level among all three. Data on its own carries no meaning. For data to become information, it must be interpreted and take on a meaning. For example, the height of Mt. Everest is generally considered as "data", a book on Mt. Everest geological characteristics may be considered as "information", and a report containing practical information on the best way to reach Mt. Everest's peak may be considered as "knowledge".

Information as a concept bears a diversity of meanings, from everyday usage to technical settings. Generally speaking, the concept of information is closely related to notions of constraint, communication, control, data, form, instruction, knowledge, meaning, mental stimulus, pattern, perception, and representation.

Beynon-Davies uses the concept of a sign to distinguish between data and information; data are symbols while information occurs when symbols are used to refer to something.[14]

It is people and computers who collect data and impose patterns on it. These patterns are seen as information which can be used to enhance knowledge. These patterns can be interpreted as truth, and are authorized as aesthetic and ethical criteria. Events that leave behind perceivable physical or virtual remains can be traced back through data. Marks are no longer considered data once the link between the mark and observation is broken.[15]

Raw data refers to a collection of numbers, characters, images or other outputs from devices to convert physical quantities into symbols, that are unprocessed. Such data is typically further processed by a human or input into a computer, stored and processed there, or transmitted (output) to another human or computer (possibly through a data cable). *Raw data* is a relative term; data processing commonly occurs by stages, and the "processed data" from one stage may be considered the "raw data" of the next.

Mechanical computing devices are classified according to the means by which they represent data. An analog computer represents a datum as a voltage, distance, position, or other physical quantity. A digital computer represents a datum as a sequence of symbols drawn from a fixed alphabet. The most common digital computers use a binary alphabet, that is, an alphabet of two characters, typically denoted "0" and "1". More familiar representations, such as numbers or letters, are then constructed from the binary alphabet.

Some special forms of data are distinguished. A computer program is a collection of data, which can be interpreted as instructions. Most computer languages make a distinction between programs and the other data on which programs operate, but in some languages, notably Lisp and similar languages, programs are essentially indistinguishable from other data. It is also useful to distinguish metadata, that is, a description of other data. A similar yet earlier term for metadata is "ancillary data." The prototypical example of metadata is the library catalog, which is a description of the contents of books.

Experimental data refers to data generated within the context of a scientific investigation by observation and recording. Field data refers to raw data collected in an uncontrolled in situ environment.

See also

- Biological data
- Data acquisition
- Data analysis
- Data cable
- Data domain
- Data element
- Data farming
- Data governance
- Data integrity
- Data maintenance
- Data management
- Data mining
- Data modeling
- Computer data processing
- Data remanence
- Data set
- Data warehouse

- Database
- Datasheet
- Environmental data rescue
- Fieldwork
- Metadata
- Scientific data archiving
- Statistics
- Datastructure

References

This article was originally based on material from the Free On-line Dictionary of Computing, which is licensed under the GFDL.

[1] Matt Dye (2001). "Writing Reports" (http://www.bris.ac.uk/Depts/DeafStudiesTeaching/dissert/Writing Reports.htm). University of Bristol. .

[2] "IEEE Computer Society Style Guide, DEF" (http://www.computer.org/portal/web/publications/styleguidedef). IEEE Computer Society.
   .

[3] "WHO Style Guide" (http://whqlibdoc.who.int/hq/2004/WHO_IMD_PUB_04.1.pdf). Geneva: World Health Organization. 2004. p. 43.
   .

[4] *The Author's Guide to Writing Air Force Flight Test Center Technical Reports.* Air Force Flight Test Center.

[5] New Oxford Dictionary of English, 1999

[6] "...in educated everyday usage as represented by the Guardian newspaper, it is nowadays most often used as a singular." http://www.eisu2.bham.ac.uk/johnstf/revis006.htm

   - "When Serving the Lord, Ministers Are Often Found to Neglect Themselves" (http://www.nytimes.com/2009/01/10/us/10religion.html). New York Times. 2009. .
   - "Investment Tax Cuts Help Mostly the Rich" (http://www.nytimes.com/2009/01/10/business/10charts.html). New York Times. 2009. .

[8] *New Oxford Dictionary of English.* 1999.

[9] Tim Johns (1997). "Data: singular or plural?" (http://www.eisu2.bham.ac.uk/johnstf/revis006.htm). . "...in educated everyday usage as represented by The Guardian newspaper, it is nowadays most often used as a singular."

[10] "Data" (http://www.askoxford.com/concise_oed/data?view=uk). *Compact Oxford Dictionary.* .

[11] "Data: singular or plural?" (http://www.eisu2.bham.ac.uk/johnstf/revis006.htm). Blair Wisconsin International University. .

[12] "Singular or plural" (http://www.nottingham.ac.uk/public-affairs/uon-style-book/singular-plural.htm). *University of Nottingham Style Book.* University of Nottingham. .

[13] "Computers and computer systems" (http://openlearn.open.ac.uk/mod/resource/view.php?id=182902). *OpenLearn.* .

   - P. Beynon-Davies (2002). *Information Systems: An introduction to informatics in organisations.* Basingstoke, UK: Palgrave Macmillan. ISBN 0-333-96390-3.
   - P. Beynon-Davies (2009). *Business information systems.* Basingstoke, UK: Palgrave. ISBN 978-0-230-20368-6.

[15] Sharon Daniel. *The Database: An Aesthetics of Dignity.*

External links

- Data is a singular noun (http://purl.org/nxg/note/singular-data) (a detailed assessment)

rue:Дата

Learning

Learning is acquiring new or modifying existing knowledge, behaviors, skills, values, or preferences and may involve synthesizing different types of information. The ability to learn is possessed by humans, animals and some machines. Progress over time tends to follow learning curves.

Human learning may occur as part of education, personal development, schooling, or training. It may be goal-oriented and may be aided by motivation. The study of how learning occurs is part of neuropsychology, educational psychology, learning theory, and pedagogy. Learning may occur as a result of habituation or classical conditioning, seen in many animal species, or as a result of more complex activities such as play, seen only in relatively intelligent animals.[1] [2] Learning may occur consciously or without conscious awareness. There is evidence for human behavioral learning prenatally, in which habituation has been observed as early as 32 weeks into gestation, indicating that the central nervous system is sufficiently developed and primed for learning and memory to occur very early on in development.[3]

Play has been approached by several theorists as the first form of learning. Children play, experiment with the world, learn the rules, and learn to interact. Vygotsky agrees that play is pivotal for children's development, since they make meaning of their environment through play.

Types of learning

Simple non-associative learning

Habituation

In psychology, habituation is an example of non-associative learning in which there is a progressive diminution of behavioral response probability with repetition stimulus. An animal first responds to a stimulus, but if it is neither rewarding nor harmful the animal reduces subsequent responses. One example of this can be seen in small song birds—if a stuffed owl (or similar predator) is put into the cage, the birds initially react to it as though it were a real predator. Soon the birds react less, showing habituation. If another stuffed owl is introduced (or the same one removed and re-introduced), the birds react to it again as though it were a predator, demonstrating that it is only a very specific stimulus that is habituated to (namely, one particular unmoving owl in one place). Habituation has been shown in essentially every species of animal, as well as the large protozoan *Stentor coeruleus*.[4]

Sensitization

Sensitization is an example of non-associative learning in which the progressive amplification of a response follows repeated administrations of a stimulus (Bell et al., 1995). An everyday example of this mechanism is the repeated tonic stimulation of peripheral nerves that will occur if a person rubs his arm continuously. After a while, this stimulation will create a warm sensation that will eventually turn painful. The pain is the result of the progressively amplified synaptic response of the peripheral nerves warning the person that the stimulation is harmful. Sensitization is thought to underlie both adaptive as well as maladaptive learning processes in the organism.

Associative learning

Associative learning is the process by which an association between two stimuli or a behavior and a stimulus is learned. The two forms of associative learning are classical and operant conditioning. In the former a previously neutral stimulus is repeatedly presented together with a reflex eliciting stimuli until eventually the neutral stimulus will elicit a response on its own. In operant conditioning a certain behavior is either reinforced or punished which results in an altered probability that the behavior will happen again. Honeybees display associative learning through the proboscis extension reflex paradigm.[5]

Operant conditioning is the use of consequences to modify the occurrence and form of behavior. *Operant conditioning* is distinguished from *Pavlovian conditioning* in that operant conditioning uses reinforcement/punishment to alter an action-outcome association. In contrast Pavlovian conditioning involves strengthening of the stimulus-outcome association.

Behaviorism is a psychological movement that seeks to alter behavior by arranging the environment to elicit successful changes and to arrange consequences to maintain or diminish a behavior. Behaviorists study behaviors that can be measured and changed by the environment. However, they do not deny that there are thought processes that interact with those behaviors (see Relational Frame Theory for more information).

Delayed discounting is the process of devaluing rewards based on the delay of time they are presented. This process is thought to be tied to impulsivity. Impulsivity is a core process for many behaviors (e.g., substance abuse, problematic gambling, OCD). Making decisions is an important part of everyday functioning. How we make those decisions is based on what we perceive to be the most valuable or worthwhile actions. This is determined by what we find to be the most reinforcing stimuli. So when teaching an individual a response, you need to find the most potent reinforcer for that person. This may be a larger reinforcer at a later time or a smaller immediate reinforcer.

Classical conditioning

The typical paradigm for classical conditioning involves repeatedly pairing an unconditioned stimulus (which unfailingly evokes a reflexive response) with another previously neutral stimulus (which does not normally evoke the response). Following conditioning, the response occurs both to the unconditioned stimulus and to the other, unrelated stimulus (now referred to as the "conditioned stimulus"). The response to the conditioned stimulus is termed a *conditioned response.* The classic example is Pavlov and his dogs. Meat powder naturally will make a dog salivate when it is put into a dog's mouth; salivating is a reflexive response to the meat powder. Meat powder is the unconditioned stimulus (US) and the salivation is the unconditioned response (UR). Then Pavlov rang a bell before presenting the meat powder. The first time Pavlov rang the bell, the neutral stimulus, the dogs did not salivate, but once he put the meat powder in their mouths they began to salivate. After numerous pairings of the bell and the food the dogs learned that the bell was a signal that the food was about to come and began to salivate when the bell was rung. Once this occurred, the bell became the conditioned stimulus (CS) and the salivation to the bell became the conditioned response (CR).

Another influential person in the world of Classical Conditioning is John B. Watson. Watson's work was very influential and paved the way for B. F. Skinner's radical behaviorism. Watson's behaviorism (and philosophy of science) stood in direct contrast to Freud. Watson's view was that Freud's introspective method was too subjective, and that we should limit the study of human development to directly observable behaviors. In 1913, Watson published the article "Psychology as the Behaviorist Views," in which he argued that laboratory studies should serve psychology best as a science. Watson's most famous, and controversial, experiment, "Little Albert," where he demonstrated how psychologists can account for the learning of emotion through classical conditioning principles.

Imprinting

Imprinting is the term used in psychology and ethology to describe any kind of phase-sensitive learning (learning occurring at a particular age or a particular life stage) that is rapid and apparently independent of the consequences of behavior. It was first used to describe situations in which an animal or person learns the characteristics of some stimulus, which is therefore said to be "imprinted" onto the subject.

Observational learning

The learning process most characteristic of humans is imitation; one's personal repetition of an observed behavior, such as a dance. Humans can copy three types of information simultaneously: the demonstrator's goals, actions, and environmental outcomes (results, see Emulation (observational learning)). Through copying these types of information, (most) infants will tune into their surrounding culture.

Play

Play generally describes behavior which has no particular end in itself, but improves performance in similar situations in the future. This is seen in a wide variety of vertebrates besides humans, but is mostly limited to mammals and birds. Cats are known to play with a ball of string when young, which gives them experience with catching prey. Besides inanimate objects, animals may play with other members of their own species or other animals, such as orcas playing with seals they have caught. Play involves a significant cost to animals, such as increased vulnerability to predators and the risk of injury and possibly infection. It also consumes energy, so there must be significant benefits associated with play for it to have evolved. Play is generally seen in younger animals, suggesting a link with learning. However, it may also have other benefits not associated directly with learning, for example improving physical fitness.

Enculturation

Enculturation is the process by which a person learns the requirements of their native culture by which he or she is surrounded, and acquires values and behaviors that are appropriate or necessary in that culture.[6] The influences which as part of this process limit, direct or shape the individual, whether deliberately or not, include parents, other adults, and peers.[6] If successful, enculturation results in competence in the language, values and rituals of the culture.[6] (compare acculturation, where a person is within a culture different to their normal culture, and learns the requirements of this different culture).

Episodic learning

Episodic learning is a change in behavior that occurs as a result of an event.[7] For example, a fear of dogs that follows being bitten by a dog is episodic learning. Episodic learning is so named because events are recorded into episodic memory, which is one of the three forms of explicit learning and retrieval, along with perceptual memory and semantic memory.[8]

Multimedia learning

Multimedia learning is where a person uses both auditory and visual stimuli to learn information (Mayer 2001). This type of learning relies on dual-coding theory (Paivio 1971).

E-learning and augmented learning

Electronic learning or e-learning is a general term used to refer to Internet-based networked computer-enhanced learning. A specific and always more diffused e-learning is mobile learning (m-learning), which uses different mobile telecommunication equipment, such as cellular phones.

When a learner interacts with the e-learning environment, it's called augmented learning. By adapting to the needs of individuals, the context-driven instruction can be dynamically tailored to the learner's natural environment. Augmented digital content may include text, images, video, audio (music and voice). By personalizing instruction, augmented learning has been shown to improve learning performance for a lifetime.[9] See also Minimally Invasive Education.

Rote learning

Rote learning is a technique which avoids understanding the inner complexities and inferences of the subject that is being learned and instead focuses on memorizing the material so that it can be recalled by the learner exactly the way it was read or heard. The major practice involved in rote learning techniques is *learning by repetition*, based on the idea that one will be able to quickly recall the meaning of the material the more it is repeated. Rote learning is used in diverse areas, from mathematics to music to religion. Although it has been criticized by some schools of thought, rote learning is a necessity in many situations.

Meaningful learning

Meaningful learning refers to the concept that the learned knowledge (lets say a fact) is fully understood by the individual and that the individual knows how that specific fact relates to other stored facts (stored in your brain that is). For understanding this concept, it is good to contrast meaningful learning with the much less desirable, rote learning. Rote learning requires only that the individual remembers the information without any regard for understanding, in other words learning by rote allows the individual to recite facts without truely understanding them. Meaningful learning, on the other hand, implies there is a comprehensive knowledge of the context of the facts learned.[10]

Informal learning

Informal learning occurs through the experience of day-to-day situations (for example, one would learn to look ahead while walking because of the danger inherent in not paying attention to where one is going). It is learning from life, during a meal at table with parents, play, exploring, etc.

Formal learning

Formal learning is learning that takes place within a teacher-student relationship, such as in a school system.

Nonformal learning

Nonformal learning is organized learning outside the formal learning system. For example: learning by coming together with people with similar interests and exchanging viewpoints, in clubs or in (international) youth organizations, workshops.

Nonformal learning and combined approaches

The educational system may use a combination of formal, informal, and nonformal learning methods. The UN and EU

A depiction of the world's oldest continually operating university, the University of Bologna, Italy

recognize these different forms of learning (cf. links below). In some schools students can get points that count in the formal-learning systems if they get work done in informal-learning circuits. They may be given time to assist international youth workshops and training courses, on the condition they prepare, contribute, share and can prove this offered valuable new insight, helped to acquire new skills, a place to get experience in organizing, teaching, etc.

In order to learn a skill, such as solving a Rubik's cube quickly, several factors come into play at once:

- Directions help one learn the patterns of solving a Rubik's cube.
- Practicing the moves repeatedly and for extended time helps with "muscle memory" and therefore speed.
- Thinking critically about moves helps find shortcuts, which in turn helps to speed up future attempts.
- The Rubik's cube's six colors help anchor solving it within the head.
    - Occasionally revisiting the cube helps prevent negative learning or loss of skill.

Tangential learning

Tangential learning is the process by which people will self-educate if a topic is exposed to them in a context that they already enjoy. For example, after playing a music-based video game, some people may be motivated to learn how to play a real instrument, or after watching a TV show that references Faust and Lovecraft, some people may be inspired to read the original work.

Dialogic learning

Dialogic learning is a type of learning based on dialogue.

Domains of learning

Benjamin Bloom has suggested three domains of learning:

- Cognitive – To recall, calculate, discuss, analyze, problem solve, etc.
- Psychomotor – To dance, swim, ski, dive, drive a car, ride a bike, etc.
- Affective – To like something or someone, love, appreciate, fear, hate, worship, etc.

These domains are not mutually exclusive. For example, in learning to play chess, the person will have to learn the rules of the game (cognitive domain); but he also has to learn how to set up the

In XXI c.

chess pieces on the chessboard and also how to properly hold and move a chess piece (psychomotor). Furthermore, later in the game the person may even learn to love the game itself, value its applications in life, and appreciate its history (affective domain).[11]

Transfer of learning

The transfer of learning can be defined as extending what has been learned in one context to new contexts. Determining if and to what extent a person can transfer their learned knowledge can be a strong indication of the quality of the learning experience itself. Effective memorization of information does not equal a meaningful learning experience, because the knowledge acquired might not be understood. The ability to understand and apply learnings, implies a deeper knowledge gained. The context of the original learning, time given to learn, motivation of learner, active participation, and progress monitoring of learning are all important factors that effect the degree to which learning is transferrable. New research within cognitive science has helped unfold the multidisciplinary nature of learning. Anthropology, linguistics, philosophy, psychology and neuroscience all play a role in learning. More importantly, these factors play a role in the level of understanding one person develops versus another person. [12]

Active learning

Active learning occurs when a person takes control of their learning experience. Since understanding information is the key aspect of learning, it is important for learners to recognize what they understand and what they do not. By doing so, they can monitor their own mastery of subjects. Active learning encourages learners to have an internal dialogue in which they are verbalizing their understandings. This and other meta- cognitive strategies can be taught to a child over time. Studies within metacognition have proven the value in active learning, claiming that the learning is usually at a stronger level as a result. [13]

Notes

[1] Jungle Gyms: The Evolution of Animal Play (http://nationalzoo.si.edu/Publications/ZooGoer/1996/1/junglegyms.cfm)

[2] What behavior can we expect of octopuses? (http://www.thecephalopodpage.org/behavior.php)

[3] Sandman, Wadhwa, Hetrick, Porto & Peeke. (1997). Human fetal heart rate dishabituation between thirty and thirty-two weeks gestation. Child Development, 68, 1031–1040.

[4] Wood, D.C. (1988). Habituation in *Stentor* produced by mechanoreceptor channel modification. *Journal of Neuroscience*, 2254 (8).

[5] Bitterman et al. 1983. Classical Conditioning of Proboscis Extension in Honeybees (*Apis mellifera*). J. Comp. Psych. 97: 107-119.

[6] Grusec, Joan E.; Hastings, Paul D. "Handbook of Socialization: Theory and Research", 2007, Guilford Press; ISBN 1-59385-332-7, 9781593853327; at page 547.

[7] Terry, W. S. (2006). Learning and Memory: Basic principles, processes, and procedures. Boston: Pearson Education, Inc.

[8] Baars, B. J. & Gage, N. M. (2007). Cognition, Brain, and Consciousness: Introduction to cognitive neuroscience. London: Elsevier Ltd.

[9] Augmented Learning (http://portal.acm.org/citation.cfm?id=1156186), Augmented Learning: Context-Aware Mobile Augmented Reality Architecture for Learning

[10] Hassard, Jack. "Backup of Meaningful Learning Model" (http://www.csudh.edu/dearhabermas/advorgbk02.htm). . Retrieved 30 November 2011.

[11] Bloom's Taxonomy of Learning (http://www.businessballs.com/bloomstaxonomyoflearningdomains.htm)

[12] [(Bransford, 2000, pg.51-78)]

[13] [(Bransford, 2000, pg.15-20)]

References

- Holt, John (1983). *How Children Learn* (http://books.google.fr/books?id=glEiAAAAMAAJ). UK: Penguin Books. ISBN 0140225706.

- Mayer, R.E. (2001). *Multimedia learning* (http://books.google.com/books?id=ymJ9o-w_6WEC). New York: Cambridge University Press. ISBN 0-52178-749-1.

- Paivio, A. (1971). *Imagery and verbal processes* (http://books.google.com/books?id=xmB9AAAAMAAJ). New York: Holt, Rinehart, and Winston.

- Vosniadou, Stella. *How Children Learn* (http://www.ibe.unesco.org/publications/EducationalPracticesSeriesPdf/prac07e.pdf). UK: UNESCO.

Online_and_offline

The terms "**online**" and "**offline**" (also stylized as "**on-line**" and "**off-line**") have specific meanings in regard to computer technology and telecommunications. In general, "online" indicates a state of connectivity, while "offline" indicates a disconnected state. In common usage, "online" often refers to the Internet or the World-Wide Web.

The concepts have however been extended from their computing and telecommunication meanings into the area of human interaction and conversation, such that even *offline* can be used in contrast to the common usage of *online*. For example, discussions taking place during a business meeting are "online", while issues that do not concern all participants of the meeting should be "taken offline" — continued outside of the meeting.

Standard definitions

In computer technology and telecommunication, **online** and **offline** are defined by Federal Standard 1037C. They are states or conditions of a "device or equipment" or of a "functional unit". To be considered online, one of the following must apply to a device:

- Under the direct control of another device
- Under the direct control of the system with which it is associated
- Available for immediate use on demand by the system without human intervention
- Connected to a system, and is in operation
- Functional and ready for service

In contrast, a device that is offline meets none of these criteria (e.g., its main power source is disconnected or turned off, or it is off-power).

Offline mail

One example of a common use of these concepts is a mail user agent that can be instructed to be in either online or offline states. One such MUA is Microsoft Outlook. When online it will attempt to connect to mail servers (to check for new mail at regular intervals, for example), and when offline it will not attempt to make any such connection. The online or offline state of the MUA does not necessarily reflect the connection status between the computer on which it is running and the Internet. That is, the computer itself may be online—connected to Internet via a cable modem or other means—while Outlook is kept offline by the user, so that it makes no attempt to send or to receive messages. Similarly, a computer may be configured to employ a dial-up connection on demand (as when an application such as Outlook attempts to make connection to a server), but the user may not wish for Outlook to trigger that call whenever it is configured to check for mail.[1]

Offline media playing

Another example of the use of these concepts is digital audio technology. A tape recorder, digital audio editor, or other device that is online is one whose clock is under the control of the clock of a synchronization master device. When the sync master commences playback, the online device automatically synchronizes itself to the master and commences playing from the same point in the recording. A device that is offline uses no external clock reference and relies upon its own internal clock. When a large number of devices are connected to a sync master it is often convenient, if one wants to hear just the output of one single device, to take it offline because, if the device is played back online, all synchronized devices have to locate the playback point and wait for each other device to be in synchronization.[2] (For related discussion, see MIDI timecode, word sync, and recording system synchronization.)

Offline browsing

A third example of a common use of these concepts is a web browser that can be instructed to be in either online or offline states. The browser attempts to fetch pages from servers while only in the online state. In the offline state, users can perform **offline browsing**, where pages can be browsed using local copies of those pages that have previously been downloaded while in the on-line state. This can be useful when the computer is offline and connection to the Internet is impossible or undesirable. The pages are downloaded either implicitly into the web browser's own cache as a result of prior online browsing by the user or explicitly by a browser configured to keep local copies of certain web pages, which are updated when the browser is in the online state, either by checking that the local copies are up-to-date at regular intervals or by checking that the local copies are up-to-date whenever the browser is switched to the on-line state. One such web browser capable of being explicitly configured to download pages for offline browsing is Internet Explorer. When pages are added to the Favourites list, they can be marked to be "available for offline browsing". Internet Explorer will download to local copies both the marked page and, optionally, all of the pages that it links to. In Internet Explorer version 6, the level of direct and indirect links, the maximum amount of local disc space allowed to be consumed, and the schedule on which local copies are checked to see whether they are up-to-date, are configurable for each individual Favourites entry.[3] [4] [5] [6]

Offline browsing known as "Offline favourites" was removed as a feature in Internet Explorer 7, which now supports only saving single web pages, but not an entire site.

Others

Likewise, offline storage is computer data storage that is not "available for immediate use on demand by the system without human intervention." Additionally, an otherwise online system that is powered down is considered offline[7]

.

Generalizations

Online and offline distinctions have been generalized from computing and telecommunication into the field of human interpersonal relationships. The distinction between what is considered online and what is considered offline has become a subject of study in the field of sociology.[8]

The distinction between online and offline is conventionally seen as the distinction between computer-mediated communication and face-to-face communication (e.g., face time), respectively. Online is virtuality or cyberspace, and offline is reality (i.e., Real life or meatspace). Slater states that this distinction is "obviously far too simple".[8] To support his argument that the distinctions in relationships are more complex than a simple online/offline dichotomy, he observes that some people draw no distinction between an on-line relationship, such as indulging in cybersex, and an offline relationship, such as being pen pals. He also argues that even the telephone can be regarded as an online experience in some circumstances, and that the blurring of the distinctions between the uses of various technologies (such as PDA and mobile phone, internet television and Internet, and telephone and Voice over Internet Protocol) has made it "impossible to use the term *on-line* meaningfully in the sense that was employed by the first generation of Internet research".[8]

Slater asserts that there are legal and regulatory pressures to reduce the distinction between online and offline, with a "general tendency to assimilate online to offline and erase the distinction," stressing, however, that this does not mean that online relationships are being reduced to *pre-existing* offline relationships. He conjectures that greater legal status may be assigned to online relationships (pointing out that contractual relationships, such as business transactions, online are already seen as just as "real" as their offline counterparts), although he states it to be hard to imagine courts awarding palimony to people who have had a purely online sexual relationship. He also conjectures that an online/offline distinction may be seen by people as "rather quaint and not quite comprehensible" within 10 years.[8]

This distinction between *online* and *offline* is sometimes inverted, with online concepts being used to define and to explain offline activities, rather than (as per the conventions of the desktop metaphor with its desktops, trash cans, folders, and so forth) the other way around. Several cartoons appearing in *The New Yorker* have satirized this. One includes Saint Peter asking for a username and a password before admitting a man into Heaven. Another illustrates "the off-line store" where "All items are actual size!" shoppers may "Take it home as soon as you pay for it!" and "Merchandise may be handled prior to purchase!"[9] [10]

See also

- Computer networking
- NLS, or the "oN-Line System"
- Offline reader
- On the fly: Computer usage
- Online and offline algorithms
- Online editing and offline editing — the online/offline distinction in video editing
- Online games
- Online identity
- Open access (publishing)
- Reputation
- Website mirroring software

References

[1] Bill Mann (2003). *How to Do Everything with Microsoft Office Outlook 2003*. McGraw-Hill Professional. pp. 76–77. ISBN 0072230703.

[2] Bill Gibson (1998). *Audiopro Home Recording Course: A Comprehensive Multimedia Audio Recording Text*. Hal Leonard. pp. 155. ISBN 0872887154.

[3] Arabella Dymoke (2004). "an a to z of internet terms". *Good Web Guide*. The Good Web Guide Ltd. pp. 17. ISBN 1903282462.

[4] Paul Heltzel (2002). "Wireless Road Tricks". *The Complete Idiot's Guide to Wireless Computing and Networking*. Alpha Books. pp. 205. ISBN 0028642872.

[5] Glen Waller and Vanessa Waller (2000). *The Internet Companion: The Easy Australian Guide*. UNSW Press. pp. 110–112. ISBN 0868404993.

[6] Brian Barber (2001). "Configuring Internet Technologies". *Configuring and Troubleshooting Windows XP Professional*. Syngress Publishing. pp. 285–389. ISBN 1928994806.

[7] http://what-is-what.com/what_is/online.html

[8] Don Slater (2002). "Social Relationships and Identity On-line and Off-line". In Leah, Sonia, Lievrouw, and Livingstone. *Handbook of New Media: Social Shaping and Consequences of ICTs*. Sage Publications Inc. pp. 533–543. ISBN 0761965106.

[9] Rosabeth Moss Kanter (2001). "Introduction". *Evolve: Succeeding in the digital culture of tomorrow*. Harvard Business School. ISBN 1578514398.

[10] The "off-line store" cartoon from *The New Yorker* (http://executiveeducation.wharton.upenn.edu/ebuzz/0508/images/cartoon2.jpg)

- ⓔ *This article incorporates public domain material from websites or documents of the General Services Administration* (in support of MIL-STD-188).

Article Sources and Contributors

Web_Inquiry_Projects *Source*: http://en.wikipedia.org/w/index.php?title=Web_Inquiry_Projects *Contributors*: Bjwebb, Burlywood, Calliopejen1, DGG, Kamezuki, Nekohakase, Rbrwr, Yakovsh, Zouf, 4 anonymous edits

San_Diego_State_University *Source*: http://en.wikipedia.org/w/index.php?title=San_Diego_State_University *Contributors*: 5 albert square, 72Dino, AKGhetto, AkiStuart, Alai, Amerique, Anand8800, Angela, Angr, Anon134, AppleRaven, Armbrust, Arpowers, Asiananimal, Asterion, Astuishin, Auntof6, BD2412, Balloonguy, Bchezbro, Billypadre, BlankVerse, Blix3, Bobblewik, Borninthteguz, Brian1078, CGameProgrammer, CaliEd, Can't sleep, clown will eat me, Catapult, Catdude, Catgut, Chainclaw, Choalbaton, Choster, Chris the speller, Cinocente, Cmdrjameson, Coasterguy, ColBog, CopperSquare, Cybercobra, D6, DARTH SIDIOUS 2, Dabackgammonator, Dale Arnett, Damienhunter, Dananderson, David Fuchs, Dbiel, Diefenbaker, Dj09ou, Djln, DocWatson42, Dynaflow, EJOlney, Edward, Edwy, ElKevbo, Elkman, Eric-Wester, Esrever, Eustress, Ezeu, FCYTravis, Falcon8765, Fitzwilliam, Florentino floro, Foolishgrunt, Freakofnurture, Freemasonx, Galwhaa, Gateman1997, Gentgeen, Geographer, Gettingtoit, Glennlowney, Greenseries23, Guitargoddanny, Hammersoft, Hawaiian717, Hmains, ILovePlankton, IRelayer, Icairns, Iridescent, Iss246, J-beda, J3ff, JHunterJ, JLaTondre, JerH, Jigen III, Johnbrownsbody, Jojhutton, Jweiss11, Kenyon, Kinaro, KnightRider, Koman90, Krichison, Ktr101, Kukini, LaszloWalrus, Law, Lawrence Cohen, Levineps, Lexus1555, Lightmouse, LilHelpa, Livajo, Loren36, Luna Santin, MER-C, MPF, Marco Guzman, Jr, Martarius, Martinp23, Masonpatriot, Mattl2001, Maxschmelling, Mchacon89, Meganfoxx, Memo@sdsu.edu, Meno25, Mentifisto, Merope, MiamiDolphins3, Mike Selinker, Minna Sora no Shita, MisfitToys, Mlaffs, Mmoneypenny, Moe Epsilon, Muhandes, Nakon, Nehrams2020, Neovu79, Netoholic, Njbob, OCNative, Ohnoitsjamie, Omicronpersei8, Ommnomnomgulp, Optigan13, PS2pcGAMER, Pacific1987, Paloma Walker, Pats1, Peruvianllama, Phlegm Rooster, Popypoed, Pstuart, Pubdog, QuiteRandom, R'n'B, Radiopathy, Rettetast, Rich Farmbrough, Rick Block, Rjwilmsi, Rkwikifan, Rm999, RoyBoy, Rsduhamel, SallyForth123, SarahKnef, Saria, ScholarlyScholar91, Scanpainter, Ser Amantio di Nicolao, Serapio, Serraqdawgjrs, Seth Ilys, Seven Days, SeventyThree, Shindotv, Shirt58, ShortRound23, SimMoonXP, SirGrant, Stepheng3, Streltzer, Student7, Summeree, Superflush, Surfacing 731, Svptxag, TEB728, THB, Tapir Terrific, Tassedethe, Tedder, Tehran Citizen, Terryn3, The undertow, The wub, Thecheesykid, Thischarmingdz08, Tktktk, Tommy2010, Tregoweth, Trekker315, Twaz, Unsuspected, ValleyWikian, Vishnava, Vossman, WJetChao, WODUP, WSUCanuck, Walkiped, WhisperToMe, Woohookitty, Xpendersx, Z1nemo, Zmfactor, Zzyzx11 the clone, 610 anonymous edits

University_of_Illinois_at_Urbana–Champaign *Source*: http://en.wikipedia.org/w/index.php?title=University_of_Illinois_at_Urbana%E2%80%93Champaign *Contributors*: Abhijitsathe, AcidFlask, Agriculture, Alarics, Albanaco, Aleenf1, Alexanderbanning, Alexbouditsky, AlexiusHoratius, Alexqw, Alfergus, AlistairMcMillan, AliveFreeHappy, Ambarish, Anaradr, AndperseAndy, Andrei Stroe, AndrewHowse, Angr, Anti-Nationalist, Ariescwliang, ArjunIyer, ArthurGD, AscendedAnathema, Astuishin, Athaphon, Atomician, Avraham, Avram, B, BD2412, Baltasaro, Beland, Benandorsqueaks, Bender235, Bhockey10, Bkonrad, BlueAzure, Boardwalk444, Bobblewik, Bobtheguy, Bogsat, Bongwarrior, Boredom12, Brholden, Brookie, Bullshark44, Bunnyhop11, Burkso2, Bvjrm, CWenger, Calabe1992, Calen11, CaliEd, Capricorn42, Cardsplayer4life, Catgut, Ceuthophilus, Ceyockey, Cgoldsmith, Champaigncvb, Chensiyuan, Chidomes08, Chipotlehero, Chitown03, Chiwara, Choster, Chowbok, Chris the speller, ClaytonHinkle, Cmdrjameson, Cmontyburns99, Coder Dan, CommonsDelinker, ComputerJA, Craigy144, Crotchety Old Man, Cumulant, DMacks, Dabomb87, Daderot, Dale Arnett, Daniel Case, DanielNuyu, Danthemankhan, Danw1226, DarkFalls, DavidA, DavidGrayson, DavidH, DerHexer, Dmoontown5, Donalds, Dori, Dpbsmith, Dputig07, Drjones2343, Drmorris75, Dsb75800, Dual Freq, Dudesleeper, EQuacquarelli, Eaolson, Ebyabe, Ecrosenberg, Edknol, Edward321, ElKevbo, Elipongo, Entry1234, Epeefleche, Erockrph, Esrever, Estrellaroja, Eustress, Evolauxia, Excirial, FairFare, Fetchcomms, Finavon, Fishyillini, Flyguy33, Fox, Frank12, Fsiler, Fumo7887, Funandtrvl, Fusionmix, Fuzheado, G3pro, Gagconcerto, Gaigeb, Gaius Cornelius, Gary Cziko, Gavreh, Gene.arboit, Giftlite, Giraffedata, Gloriamarie, Gopherbone, Goplat, Gpetrov, Grammaticus Repairo, Grey Wanderer, Grfnkmp, Grillini, Grsz11, Gshirts, Gtrmp, H Padleckas, H.al-shawaf, Habitually Broken, HalloweenHJB, HappyCamper, Hoary, Hollis1138, HoundofBaskersville, HuskyHuskie, I dream of horses, IceCreamAntisocial, Illinifan(david), Illinifan2, Illinimax, Indigo7, InsaneNewman, Island Monkey, Islandemcee, Isota.s, J-beda, J.delanoy, J450NH3, JDoorjam, Jacbo the Rocket Boy, Jacqui M, JamesAM, Jamest630, Jaucourt, Jawed, Jbues, Jcarlyle, Jccort, Jennavecia, Jfultz, Jhumbo, JillandJack, Jivecat, Jkuofi, Jllm06, Joel Steinfeldt, John, JohnInDC, JoshG, Juliancolton, Justinm1978, Jweiss11, Kaihsu, Kakomu, Kamuichikap, Karenh3, Katsis, Keeper76, Keltus, Kevyn, Khueviet, King Pickle, Koavf, Kstingily, Ktr101, Ktsquare, Kubigula, Laissezfaire2k, LaszloWalrus, Lcurvey, Le Deluge, Lesgles, Levineps, Lhakthong, Libertyville, Lightmouse, Lizzisansc, Lkozuch, Loggie, LonelyBeacon, Lova Falk, Lowellian, MVillani1985, Mach3moe, Madcoverboy, Magioladitis, Mahatma42, Marco Guzman, Jr, Markb, Marshu, Martinguerre, Masonpatriot, Masterpiece2000, MaxVeers, Maximus Rex, McCart42, Mcgrady635, Mcshadypl, Mdeliberto, Meelar, Mendaliv, Mephistophelian, Merumerume, Mgromowsky, MichaelDavidSmith, Miha901, Mikebrand, Mikecngan, Mikefall2, Minghong, Minna Sora no Shita, Minnecologies, Mkresca, Mobius, Modelun88, Moe Epsilon, Moncrief, Mrgates, Mrjohns2, Mrquizzical, Myasuda, Myk60640, Mypurplepassionfruit, N5iln, NSR, NThomas, Natalie Erin, Ndonohue, Newyorxico, Nishkid64, No Hollaback Girl, Noah Salzman, Nsk92, ONEder Boy, Ohio12345, Oleg Alexandrov, Optikos, Oxymoron83, PDE, PDH, Paerra, Parallel or Together?, Pbell87, Pentawing, Perry753, Peter Horn, Petero9, Petter Strandmark, Pharaoh of the Wizards, Phuzion, PiMaster3, Pink Bull, Plastikspork, Presidentman, Psk10, Qchristensen, Qst, RBXguy, Racepacket, RadicalBender, Ragib, Raystorm, Razorback216, Razvan NEAGOE, Recognizance, Retired username, Rich Farmbrough, Richardsur, Rixnixon, Rjwilmsi, Rkevins, Rlhindle, Rogerd, Rossar, Rossi101, Rreagan007, RyanGerbil10, SEWilco, SamAMac, Samuel, Samw, Sarregouset, SeanMack, Searing, Senator Palpatine, Seth Ilys, Sevilledade, ShakingSpirit, ShareHare, Shelffan, Siddhartha 90, Sjhshh, Slagestee, Slo-mo, Smallbones, Smilingsuzy, Snpoj, Some people, SpacePope, Spellcast, Splash, Sporkielols123, Squideshi, Squinky too, Ssgmcwatson, Steinpal, Stjimmy2311, Stmoore1, Sumit Dutta, Sup80377, Superdosh, Superflush, SystemBuilder, Szyslak, THEunique, TJRScudieri, Tammynicastro, Tb, Tbakas2, Tbhotch, Tdonohue, Tdowling, Teamjenn, Teemu08, Terryn3, That Guy, From That Show!, The Random Editor, The wub, TheAznSensation, TheBeastie, TheCatalyst31, TheChief, TheParanoidOne, Thesilverbail, Thesquire, Thingg, Tiddly Tom, Tim Ross, Toddst1, Tone.itdown1901, Tool2Die4, TreasuryTag, Trialsanderrors, Triwbe, Tsunade, Ukexpat, Uoflguy, Updatehelper, Upholder, Uppland, UrukHaiLoR, Utopianheaven, Valfontis, Vandymorgan, Vbgamer45, Vbvbvbvbvb, Victoriaedwards, Wachholder, Wachholder0, Warden42, WhisperToMe, WikiKingOfMishawaka, Wordbuilder, WorldAtlas, Wschrive, Wycislo, Xiahou, Xingdo44, Yamamoto Ichiro, Ynhockey, Yoyoyoshia, Zamland, Zanter, Zereshk, Zoe, Zoicon5, הסרפד, 1218 anonymous edits

Information *Source*: http://en.wikipedia.org/w/index.php?title=Information *Contributors*: "alyosha", 5 albert square, A. B., A520, AJackl, Aesopos, Al Lemos, Alan Liefting, Alansohn, Alasdair, Ale jrb, Alex.muller, Algorithms, Alphabravotango, Alphax, Amerique, Ancheta Wis, Andres, Andrewbadr, Andrewrp, Andrewrutherford, AndriesVanRenssen, AndriuZ, Anne11jun, Antandrus, Apurvasukant, Ariaconditzione, Ariedartin, Arman Cagle, Arthur Rubin, Asterisk98, Atroche, Auntof6, Avs5221, BD2412, Bart v M, Bbarkley, Bebenko, Beetstra, Ben-Zin, Bensaccount, Bertilvidet, BigDunc, Billreid, BirgerH, Blakkandekka, Bluerasberry, Bobblewik, Bongwarrior, Boxplot, Bradshow, Brian Dare, Brianjd, Browneze, BryanD, Bubba73, Bueller 007, CALR, CES1596, CIreland, COMPATT, COMPFUNK2, CRGreathouse, Calieber, Can't sleep, clown will eat me, Capricorn42, CardinalDan, Carlroller, Cassie, Catinator, Celcom, Cenarium, Chamal N, CharlesC, Chithrapriya, Chitvamasi, Choster, Christian List, Christopher Parham, Ciaran H, Ckatz, Cmsreview, Cobi, Cocomo-jp, Complete, Conversion script, Coywish, Crystallina, Csharpboy, Cuckoofridge, Cyan, Cyfal, D6, DalaoDy, Daniel.Cardenas, Danny lost, Daven200520, David Eppstein, David0811, Dawnseeker2000, Dehneshin, Delldot, Deltabeignet, Denisarona, Denisutku, DerHexer, Dessimoz, Dessources, Diagonalfish, Dicklyon, Djmiller9975, Dorkysnorky123654, Download, Downtownee, Draccon136, Dreadstar, Dreap, Dreftymac, Dungsff, Eaefremov, EagleFan, Edgerunner76, Ellywa, Eloquence, Em3ryguy, EndlessWorld, Enigma55, Epbr123, EugeneZelenko, Eurobas, Everyking, Excirial, Exformation, Fabrício Kury, Faustnh, Feinoha, Flammifer, FlavrSavr, Flcelloguy, Floridi, Fredrik, Frosted14, Fæ, GEBStgo, Galois17, Gamma2delta, GaryColemanFan, Gbbinning, Ged UK, GeeJo, George100, Gfoley4, Giftlite, Goatasaur, God of Slaughter, Gogo Dodo, Golgofrinchian, GrayFullbuster, Gregbard, Grm wnr, Gscshoyru, Gtg204y, Haham hanuka, HalfShadow, Hallenrm, Hard Sin, Harmeetkaur09, Helix84, Hephaestos, Hesar, Hot torew, Hsarkka, Iancarter, Igiffin, In4matt, Incnis Mrsi, Indon, InformationZone, Informatwr, InverseHypercube, Iridescent, Iseecubes, Isria, Ivan Štambuk, Ixfd64, J.delanoy, J04n, JFreeman, JLaTondre, Jakehall2, Jasonlums, Jayarathina, Jdunn0101, Jebba, Jerrch, Jheald, Jimothytrotter, JinJian, Joeblakesley, Johnuniq, Jon Awbrey, JonesC-NC, Jorfer, Jose77, Joyous!, Jpgordon, Juliancolton, Jusjih, Just plain Bill, Jwdietrich2, Jwithers, K50 Dude, KYPark, Kby, Kentback, Kevinmon, Kgeza7, Khalid Mahmood, Khobler, Kimberleyhastly, Kimse, King of Hearts, Kirkjames, Kjells, Kku, Klausness, Ksanyi, Kuru, Kvng, Kyle Barbour, Kyle J Moore, La goutte de pluie, Lalalalalala, Ldonna, Leandrod, Leonariso, Levineps, Lexor, Linshukun, Lir, Little guru, Logan, LogicalDash, LonelyMarble, Loom91, Loren.wilton, Lotje, Lottamiata, LtNOWIS, Luapnampahc, Luvstar 17, M.boli, MC MasterChef, MER-C, MK8, Maashatra11, Machine Elf 1735, Magdalena Szarafin, Magister Mathematicae, MagnaMopus, Mah Nah, Manuel Trujillo Berges, Maria Vargas, Mark Renier, MarsRover, Martpol, Masgatotkaca, Materialscientist, Maurice Carbonaro, Mayooranathan, Mdebets, Meelar, Meeples, Mentifisto, Michael Fourman, Michael Hardy, Michaelschmatz, Michal Jurosz, Mike J B, Mike Rosoft, MikeGasser, Mikeblas, Millahnna, MisterSheik, Mjb, Mkoval, Mmalbayrakoğlu, Modster, Montag451, Mpfrank, Mr Stephen, Mr.Z-man, Mtz07, My mom is cool, NAHID, Naudefj, NawlinWiki, Nelbathy, Neo-Jay, Neparis, Nilmerg, Nixdorf, Njaelkies Lea, Nosferatütr, Obeattie, Oberst, Ohnoitsjamie, Oicumayberight, Olathe, OleMaster, Olivier, Omnipaedista, Ott, Overix, PGWG, PKT, PaulHanson, Peak, Pelister, Pepve, PeterSymonds, Peterdjones, Philip Trueman, PhnomPencil, Piano non troppo, Pinkcyberheart, Pir, PlatonicIdeas, Pointillist, Poojamal, Poor Yorick, Pooryorick, Pratibha sharma, Prickus, Pvalozic, Pvm 02, R'n'B, R.Dhiyanesh, Ramobear, Ranveig, Rasmus Faber, Rattle, RexNL, Riana, Richard001, RichardF, Rizeg70, Rlitwin, Robert W. Wright, Roberto Gejman, Robinh, Robocracy, Romanm, Roxonfh, Rronline, Rspanton, Ruud Koot, ST47, SWAdair, Samanwith, Samboy, Sbamyani, Scope creep, Sct72, Sean.hoyland, Securiger, Semmelweiss, Sesel, ShadowRangerRIT, Shahidislam31, Sheizaf, Shindo9Hikaru, Shizhao, Silence, Simoes, Sir Nicholas de Mimsy-Porpington, SkepticalMetal, SkyMachine, Smartse, Smooth O, Smyth, Snowded, Solitude, Spinningspark, Spot, Sputnikcccp, Sssbbbrrr, Stebbins, SteinbDJ, Steipe, Stephenb, Stereotek, Stevenson-Perez, Stevertigo, Svetovid, Systemetsys, Systemizer, THF, Tad Lincoln, Taxisfolder, Tbhotch, Tcsetattr, Terence, Terrifictriffid, TestPilot, The Anome, TheAMmollusc, TheKMan, Thedosmann, Thingg, Think outside the box, Thomasda, Thriceplus, Tide rolls, Timir Saxa, Tnxman307, Tobias Bergemann, Togo, TomasBat, Tomos, Tpbradbury, Trevor MacInnis, Tritium6, Truman Burbank, Unmerklich, Vaishalimathur14, Vald, Versageek, Versus22, Vespristiano, Vishal.belawade, Voyagerfan5761, Wavelength, Wigren, Wikiborg, Wikieditor06, Wikiwlod, Wile E. Heresiarch, Wingsandsword, Wlodzimierz, Woohookitty, WpZurp, Xaphnir, Xdamr, Xyzzyplugh, YankeeDoodle14, Yekrats, Yettie0711, Yidisheryid, Yuma en, Z.E.R.O., Zarcadia, Zondor, Zzuuzz, Александър, 707 anonymous edits

Data *Source*: http://en.wikipedia.org/w/index.php?title=Data *Contributors*: 192.75.241.xxx, 208.245.214.xxx, A.M.Lewis, Aadal, Aarktica, Abramjackson, Achaemenes II, Acronymsical, Adam M. Gadomski, Aditya, AdjustShift, Adrian J. Hunter, Ahoerstemeier, Alasdair, Aldie, Aldrichg, Aleenf1, Alexius08, AlistairMcMillan, Amd628, Andrew Levine, AndrewHowse, Angrytoast, Antandrus, Apollo, Arikanari, Aroundthewayboy, Arthena, Arthur Rubin, Astral, Atif.t2, Avoided, Beetstra, Begewe, Beyondthislife, Bhadani, Bikeable, Blake Burba, Blue Hoopy Frood, Bluemask, Bluerasberry, Bobo192, Bomac, Bongwarrior, Boxplot, Bped1985, Bpilstrom, COMPATT, COMPFUNK2, CRGreathouse, Calabe1992, Calvin 1998, Capricorn42, Ccloudies, Cenarium, Christopher Denman, Chuunen Baka, Clenny93, Coemgenus, Colincbn, Connectel, Conversion script, Cool moe dee 345, Corpx, Corti, Cpiral, Cpl Syx, CustardJack, Cybercobra, DJDunsie, Daniel.Cardenas, DanielDeibler, Dar-Ape, Daven200520, Dawnseeker2000, Dcljr, Decltype, Deflective, DerHexer, Dfletter, Dhaluza, Djkernen, Dmarquard, Dmccreary,

Image Sources, Licenses and Contributors

Printed by Books on Demand GmbH, Norderstedt / Germany